Organization
Transformation Theorists
and
Practitioners

Organization Transformation Theorists and Practitioners

PROFILES AND THEMES

Beverly R. Fletcher

Westport, Connecticut
London

Library of Congresss Cataloging-in-Publication Data

Fletcher, Beverly R.
    Organization transformation theorists and practitioners : profiles
and themes / Beverly R. Fletcher.
       p. cm.
    Includes bibliographical references.
    ISBN 0–275–93584–1 (Alk. paper)
    1. Organizational change.   I. Title.
HD58.8.F55   1990
658.4′06—dc20   90–34367

British Library Cataloguing-in-Publication Data is available.

Library of Congress Catalog Card Number: 90–34397
ISBN: 0–275–93584–1

First published in 1990

Praeger Publishers, 88 Post Road West, Westport, CT 06881
An imprint of Greenwood Publishing Group, Inc.

Printed in the United States of America

The paper used in this book complies with the
Permanent Paper Standard issued by the National
Information Standards Organization (Z39.48–1984).

10 9 8 7 6 5 4

To my sons and daughter:
Victor, Mark, and Michelle Parker;
it is indeed symbolic that nothing is impossible.

Contents

Figure and Tables

Figure

Tables

Preface

During the past decade, organizational observers have become painfully aware of the dramatic impact rapidly changing environmental conditions are making on organizations. Various economic, cultural, and social trends have combined to create a critical need for theories and practices that aid large-scale, transformative changes in organizations. Transformative changes in cultural, religious, legal, political, social, and business environments are making previously successful organizational practices and strategies ineffective. According to Moore and Gergen (1988), nearly all U.S. organizations will be going through five-to-twenty years of major rapid changes as world economies adapt to a new societal order. This includes business, government, community, human service, and educational organizations—it affects us all.

History has shown that every age has had to develop organizational forms that are appropriate to that age if those organizations are to survive and develop. Accordingly, today's organizations must develop the ability and flexibility to continually adjust and adapt to rapidly changing environments if they are to survive and prosper in today's world. Organizations are being forced to either transform their assumptions, values, structures, and processes in appropriate ways or cease to exist.

There are significant new trends in the composition of U.S workers. They are increasingly becoming older, better educated, more culturally and ethnically diverse, more gender-balanced, and more focused on "quality-of-life" issues. Trends such as revolutionary changes in the prevailing scientific view of knowledge and reality are having a profound impact on organization theory and practice. Signs of fundamental changes in the belief structures of Western societies include an expansion of scientific epistemological and ontological assumptions to embrace radically different concepts such as human consciousness. These concepts have been historically ignored by the scientific community because they do not fit a scientific paradigm that insists on "objectivity." When we add to all this the current worldwide economy and global competition, it is easy to see why U.S. organizations are being forced to make changes critical to their fundamental natures.

There is, indeed, a pressing need for all organizations to use methods and theories that will help them effectively transform themselves to meet today's challenges. Organization Transformation (OT) is a new area of theory and practice that has emerged to help organizations meet the critical need to transform. OT involves transforming the purposes, structures, cultures, and strategies of organizations. The purpose of this book is to explore Organization Transformation by studying selected individuals who are developing and applying it. The focus is specifically on theorists and practitioners of Organization Transformation. Why look at practitioners and theorists rather than focus directly on the phenomenon itself? The answer to this question lies in certain philosophical assumptions about the nature of reality and the grounds of knowledge. This book's basic assumption is that there is intrinsic value to exploring the OT phenomenon from the point of view of people who are part of its practice and theory. Therefore, the research paradigm most useful for such an inquiry is necessarily "qualitative," and this study involves methods that develop from a special in-depth personal understanding of the phenomenon. Sixteen professionals (theorists and practitioners of OT) were interviewed, and data collected from fourteen of these interviews are used in this book.

Organization Transformation theorists and practitioners are currently addressing the need to assist organizations through critical transformations. The need to develop and understand Organization Transformation theory and practice is, therefore, crucial. True knowledge begins with an understanding of the motives and assumptions of current OT theorists and practitioners. The strategy of exploring this brand new area of theory and practice by studying those who are developing and applying it has implications not only for the theorists and practitioners of Organization Transformation, but also for business firms, governmental departments and agencies, community organizations, human service establishments, and educational organizations in need of assistance with their own transformations.

A GENERAL DEFINITION OF OT

Organization Transformation can be defined as a holistic, ecological, humanistic approach to radical, revolutionary change in the entire context of an organization's system. OT involves transformative changes in the fundamental nature of the organization in relation to its ecosystem and requires completely new ways of thinking, behaving, and perceiving by members of the organization. OT strategies can help an organization to be flexible and responsive to its internal and external environments. OT strategies, therefore, tend to intensify the organization's social consciousness and accordingly transform the organization's vision and mission (Levy and Merry, 1986).

The basic questions asked by this study were: Who are these people? What are their underlying philosophical assumptions? What do they have in common that makes them an identifiable group of theorists and practitioners? On what points do they vary or differ? What do they think are the important contributions of OT? What impact do they predict OT will have on organizations? Thus, the purpose of the investigation was to examine OT from the inside out, emphasizing the participants' organizational concepts, beliefs, values, and practices. The various themes that emerged from this were then analyzed. A main theme running throughout the study that links the present group of OT-oriented professionals is their repeated reference to an important aspect of Organization Transformation transcending quantitative explanation. Some of them call it "energy," some "joy," and others "spirit."

Acknowledgments

I gratefully acknowledge the contribution of Bob Johnston and Michelle Parker, who brilliantly assisted in the compilation and reduction of the enormous amounts of data. I thank my friends and confidants Veda Adrus, Maralyn Ramsay, and Shirley Ladd; their faith and love were unwavering. I also thank my mentor and friend, Norma Jean Anderson, without whose support this work would not exist. I also thank George Henderson, Horace Reed, Robert Marx, and Benjamin Olayinka Akande for their willingness to comb through the many pages and various versions of my manuscript and contribute valuable feedback. In addition, I thank Sally Habana-Hafner, Conny LaFarriere, and Ed McCreanor, who listened well, understood, and gave helpful suggestions.

Finally, my appreciation and thanks go to the sixteen participants in this study, who so willingly and graciously gave of their valuable time: John D. Adams, Norma Jean Anderson, Jean Bartunek, Michael Burkart, Donald K. Carew, Katharine Esty, Allen Gordon, Evangelina Holvino, Grant Ingle, Robert W. Johnston, William G. Kueppers, Harrison Owen, Bryant Rollins, Michael Shandler, John Simmons, and Shirley Stetson-Kessler.

Organization Transformation Theorists and Practitioners

1

An Introduction to Organization Transformation

The published literature on Organization Transformation (OT), a newly emerging field of organizational theory and practice, is indeed very new and limited. At the time this study was begun, it included only eight books. The purpose of this chapter is to summarize what has been revealed by this literature about Organization Transformation: its history, theoretical foundations, and assumptions. This in turn will provide a framework for the discussion of what is *not* yet known about OT.

HISTORICAL PERSPECTIVE

Although Organization Transformation has a very short history, it appears to be increasingly capturing the interest of managers, consultants, and academicians. The current literature contains very few historical accounts of the inception or evolution of organization transformation. However, according to Johnston (1979), many Organization Development practitioners were using concepts similar to those which are now thought to comprise Organization Transformation theory as early as 1965 and perhaps even earlier. While it is not clear exactly who coined the term, "Organization Transformation," in 1984 John Adams wrote:

I became committed to working on the problems and potentialities . . . in the context of work and organizations. I began referring to this work as Organizational Transformation (OT) in contrast to Organizational Development (OD) (in which I had been trained in graduate school in the 1960s). (Adams, 1984, p. vii)

Thus, it appears that OT evolved out of the practice of Organization Development (OD) to fill unmet needs and address situations and conditions that were not being satisfactorily attended to by existing organization theory and practice. Recently, Kilmann and Covin (1988) have stated that there is a pressing need to rejuvenate the methods and vision of OD as organizations are forced to transform themselves into adaptive, innovative, market-driven systems in order to survive and prosper in a highly competitive, global environment.

Most of the studies reviewed conclude that constantly changing environmental conditions create a need for large-scale, transformative changes within most organizations, as well as a need for new approaches to organization theory and practice. This is certainly true for the organizations described by Beres and Musser (1988), Harris (1983), Hayes and Watts (1986), Kilmann and Covin (1988), Levy and Merry (1986), Moore and Gergen (1988), and Owen (1984). Much of the literature focuses on recent societal changes throughout the world which have in turn affected most human organizations. This new wave of organization change sometimes compared to that which occurred during the Industrial Revolution, has been given many different labels, including "future shock," "the information era," "the postindustrial age," "the metaindustrial revolution," "the super industrial revolution," "the global economy," "the new order," "the new wave," and "the new age." According to Kilmann and Covin (1988), the OT movement is an outgrowth of a new global economic perspective.

Harrison Owen (1984) is one of many authors who has written about the turbulent environmental changes. He states that currently emerging turbulent environmental conditions are forcing transformation upon all organizations. Organization leaders must either transform their institutions in ways responsive to the emergent environment or cease to exist. Owen compared contemporary organizations to dinosaurs. Their anatomy and physiology are inappropriate to the emergent world. From this perspective, Organization Transformation practitioners are "facilitators" of transformation, and their process of facilitation is analogous to "midwifing" the birth of new organizational forms.

Putting environmental changes into a historical perspective, Beres and Musser (1988) write that many formal organizations were faced with cataclysmic changes when society moved from an agricultural era into the industrial age. During the Industrial Revolution, many organizations failed to meet the demands of the new age, and those that did not adjust appropriately ceased to exist. Some futurists are currently predicting that we are on the brink of a wave of change at least as dramatic and perhaps even more so. In this regard, Hayes and Watts (1986) have described what they call a "super industrial revolution" that will require fundamental changes in the basic structures of organizations. Two concepts that parallel this idea are Philip Harris's (1983) "metaindustrial revolution" and Moore and Gergen's (1988) "new world order."

Harris postulates that the macroculture of the larger society has a great impact on the microculture of its organizations. That is, the ethos of an organization is culture-bound, and the currently accelerating global social changes are becoming a driving force for organizational transformation. Harris refers to the resulting combination of profound transitions as a metaindustrial revolution. In a similar vein, Moore and Gergen (1988) write about what they call a "new world order":

Our view is that most corporations will find themselves undergoing anywhere from five-to-twenty years of serial transition as our economy adjusts to a new world order. This macroshift is driven by both new technology and foreign competition. It appears to us to be of a magnitude on the order of the industrial revolution of the last century. (p. 369)

Responding to the need to help organizations transform and adapt to their turbulent environments, many OD consultants have begun to practice what is now known as Organization Transformation. At least one professional OT network has been started in New England, and OT appears to be gaining greater acceptance as organizations react to the realities of the world marketplace. Two separate conferences on Organization Transformation have already taken place in the 1980s. The first symposium, held in New Hampshire in 1984 (Levy and Merry, 1986), produced the first comprehensive text on the subject of Organization Transformation: *Transforming Work*, edited by John Adams. The second conference occurred in October 1986, and was sponsored by the Program in Corporate Culture at the Joseph M. Katz Graduate School of Business at the University of Pittsburgh. This second conference culminated in yet another book on OT (Kilmann and Covin, 1988).

DEFINITIONS, CONCEPTS, AND THEORIES

Acknowledging the need for the development of theory along with practice, Kilmann and Covin (1988) admonish U.S. OT practitioners that there is a critical need for both in helping organizations to make major transformations effectively and efficiently. Without a sound knowledge-base to aid in transformations, American companies will experience severe psychological and economic hardships when competing with companies in other developed countries. This is especially relevant when comparing U.S. organizations with those in Germany and Japan.

Contrary to the proclamations of some of its proponents, Organization Transformation is not a clear-cut discipline (Adams, 1984). Judging from the literature, there is no universally accepted theory of OT among OT theorists and practitioners; however, among the several metaphors and descriptors for OT, some commonalities include a systems perspective and the idea of continuous transformation. We will briefly review some of the new metaphors and descriptors for OT.

A New Systems Perspective

Many OT authors advocate a holistic systems perspective. These authors include more environmental variables than usual in their systems models. Buckley and Perkins (1984) noted that a new systems perspective is emerging to deal with the complexities of social and technological innovations and that this involves a paradigm shift. They define a paradigm shift as a profound change in the thoughts, values, and perceptions that form a particular vision of reality. This newly emerging paradigm shift is conceptualized by Buckley and Perkins as a "holistic-ecological systems perspective" in which the universe is an indivisible harmonious whole. This particularly important concept emphasizes the fundamental interdependence and interrelatedness of all phenomena. Currently, this new perspective is beginning to alter the way organizations are viewing change. For example, organization change is no longer seen as a simple, compartmentalized process. It is not viewed as a single act, but as a set of complex and dynamic interactions that transform both the organization and the individuals involved into new social configurations. Gemmill and Smith (1985) also speak of the emergence of a new holistic systems viewpoint and cite the theorists who have contributed to this concept. Germmill and Smith contend that:

Changes that have had a lasting effect, come via whole-system change rather than through step-by-step processes. . . . In the context of . . . modern organization theory, this whole-system change is a prevalent theme. It is central to the organizational learning models of Argyris and Schon . . . to Golombiewski, Billingsley, and Yeager's . . . notion of gamma change within organizational development, to Sheldon's description of paradigmatic change, Davis's . . . description of contextual change, and Miller and Friesen's research . . . on quantum vs. piecemeal change. A common thread among all these modern approaches (and also one prevalent in Lewin's pioneering works) is that such change is most often induced by system jolts, turbulent environmental conditions, or internal conflicts, all of which act as catalysts for the profound transformations that take place (pp. 752–753).

New Metaphors

Out of the holistic-ecological systems perspective described by Buckley and Perkins as well as Gemmill and Smith have emerged new ways of talking about organizations. One of the more prevalent new metaphors has been used by Philip Harris (1985), who calls organizations "energy exchange systems." He defines an energy exchange system as one in which the inputs are physical, material, and psychic. In his view, organizations become dynamic human systems with life cycles in the sense that they grow, expand, develop, stabilize, decline, and eventually disappear—unless they are continually revitalized through transformation. A change process that he labels "planned renewal" takes place through the facilitation of skilled transformers who assist the organization through its reframing and retrenchment processes.

Gareth Morgan (1986), utilizing a concept similar to Buckley and Perkins' holistic-ecological systems perspective, describes organizations as "flux and transformation." This particular metaphor is just one of several used by Morgan, who states that organizations can initiate major transformations in the social ecology to which they belong by asserting their identities. An organization's identity is critical to its survival and can either cause its destruction or create conditions that will allow it to evolve along with its external environment. Morgan labels organizations "ego-centric" when they try to survive by relying mainly on the preservation of a fixed and narrowly defined identity rather than on the evolution of a more open and fluid identification with the larger ecosystem to which they belong. It is important for any organization to appreciate its systemic interdependence by recognizing that its labor force, suppliers, market, community, and even its competitors are parts of the same system.

A New Paradigm

Some authors describe the emergence of OT as a paradigm shift. For example, Peter B. Vaill (1984) writes:

Organizational Transformation (OT) means change in thought and action at a much more fundamental level than has been accomplished so far by most change agents. Since Kuhn (1970), we have used the word "paradigm" to refer to the deeper organizing principles which undergird everyday action. OT very probably *is* a paradigm shift for thinking about organizations and influencing them. (p. 18)

Vaill refers to OT as a many-dimensioned impulse that cuts across existing goals, roles, problem statements, and institutions. From this perspective, OT is something much more than a new label for the same old methods and problems. Indeed, the new paradigm's greatest power is that it deals with issues on the leading edge of social change theory. It deals with the issues and anomalies that matter—issues such as ethics, feelings, community, the human spirit, and the implications of Homo sapiens' fascination with technology, exploitation, and destruction.

Edward Lawler (1988) also has written about paradigm shifts in organizations. He developed a model that predicts the probability of paradigm shifts within organizations in the United States. Drawing upon his data, he unequivocally states that predictions about paradigm shifts can be made with a high degree of accuracy if we know such particulars about an organization as its age, performance relative to its competitors, technologies, products, and services, interacting environments, and the level of investment in the existing paradigm. In short, we must know the organization as well as a mother knows her child.

Continuous Radical Change

One of the earlier writings on the subject of Organization Transformation is by Gerald J. Skibbins (1974), who describes the process of transformation as a "radical change." Skibbins defines radical change as a large-scale, high-speed process that occurs within a single entity, a process analogous to that which occurs in caterpillars metamorphosing into butterflies, mycelia into mushrooms, and tadpoles into frogs. The entity is consequently transformed into something completely different. First it changes from state A to a completely different state, B. But unlike the familiar metamorphoses in nature, radical organization change is continuous. That is, the organization must move from state A to state B to states C, D, E, and so on in an infinite metamorphosing.

Harrison Owen (1987) states that Organization Transformation is an organization's search for a better way to be. The foremost catalyst for transformation is usually a radically altered environment in which the old ways of conducting business are no longer effective and prior forms, ways of being, and structures are no longer functional for optimum survival. Therefore, the organization is forced to change or become extinct. Since transformation is not something that the organization usually initiates without such a catalytic condition, the process is always painful. Owen compares the transformational process to the death of a life form—marking the end of an old way of being—and the emergence of a new form. Like Skibbins, he states that the process does not end with the emergence of a new form, but that it involves a continual flow from one form to another:

Although the results of transformation appear with the emergence of new organizational form, the essence of transformation lies in the odyssey or passage of the human Spirit as it moves from one formal manifestation to another. The word 'transformation' says as much, for the central idea is movement across or through forms. (p. 6)

Other Descriptions and Definitions of OT

Many writers have attempted to describe or define OT. Beckhard (1988) describes it as "a change in the shape, structure, nature of something" (p. 89). He uses this definition as the basis for a discussion of transformational change: currently all types of organizations are facing an increasing need to change their character and shape in order to survive in their respective turbulent environments.

Levy and Merry (1986) also describe OT as a radical, total change:

Organization Transformation deals with a radical, basic total change in an organization, in contrast with improving the organization and developing it or some of its parts. . . . Organizational Transformation is on the cutting edge of science. It is in the forefront of the field of organizations, and draws insights and ideas from pioneering innovative thinking in such other sciences as physics, chemistry, biology, and psychology. It is an exciting, thrilling, mindblasting subject to deal with. The mind is opened to possibilities and vistas hardly dreamed of before. Transformation deals with topics and concepts that touch on the very core and essence of human existence and being. It deals with core processes, spirituality, consciousness, creativity, and evolution. It applies approaches such as changing myths and rituals, envisioning and creating new paradigms, energizing, and raising consciousness. (p. ix)

In more traditional terms, Kilman and Covin (1988) state that Organization Transformation is a process in which organizations evaluate "what they were, what they are, what they will need to be, and how to make the necessary changes" (p. xiii). This concept of transformation is different from the usual idea of change because, in contrast to a linear extrapolation from the past, it describes a fundamental change in nature. Thus, mere knowledge of past events cannot by itself properly guide one in responding to transformative changes. Like many of the other authors, Kilmann and Covin view transformation as a systemwide process that requires completely new ways of behaving, thinking, and perceiving, by all members of the organization.

Tushman, Newman, and Nadler (1988) describe Organization Transformation as "discontinuous" or "frame-breaking change." Discontinuous and frame-breaking change involves sharp, simultaneous changes in controls, power, strategy, and structure. Generally, transformational change happens in response to, or in anticipation of, major environmental upheavals such as shifts in an organization's product life cycle, or discontinuities in its industry. Because frame-breaking changes are revolutionary, they require more than mere incremental adjustments—they reshape the entire nature of the organization. The facilitation of frame-breaking change requires substantial conceptual, social, technical, and visionary skills. This is not a task for the timid or the unskilled.

Levels and Types of Change

In an attempt to better understand the concept of Organization Transformation, many authors make a distinction between various kinds and levels of change. Perkins and Buckley (1985) state that to better understand the dynamics of Organization Transformation, it is helpful to differentiate between change and transformation. Change, they postulate, is a mere modification of behaviors, beliefs, and attitudes. This is analogous to moving from one location in a building to another location on the same floor. In contrast, transformation is a profound fundamental change in action and thought that involves an irreversible discontinuity in the status quo. The experience of transformation can be compared to moving from one building to another. These authors state, as do so many others, that transformative change usually occurs as a response to some catalyst in the organization's environment.

Watzlawick (1974) conceptualizes two different types of change: first-order and second-order. First-order change occurs within a unit of a system that itself remains basically unchanged, while second-order change is a change in the total system. Levy and Merry (1986) have also discussed first- and second-order change. They define first-order change as minor adjustments and improvements that do not affect a system's core. These kind of changes occur naturally as a system grows and develops. In contrast, second-order change (which is synonymous with Organization Transformation) is defined as: "A multidimensional, multi-level, qualitative, discontinuous, radical organizational change involving a paradigmatic shift" (p. 5).

Johnston (1987) adds a third level to organization-change theory: third-order change. Third-order change, according to Johnston, entails a permanent change in the consciousness of an organization, which facilitates making appropriate first- and second-order changes. He states that all organization transformations involve change, but not all change involves transformation. Using a simpler construction, Buckley and Perkins (1984) also write about three levels of change: minor, major, and transformative. A minor change involves a modification of behaviors and attitudes without a shift in perception. Therefore, such changes evolve around surface issues and avoid any threats to deep-seated beliefs and values—the organization remains relatively unchanged. A major change occurs when an organization develops a new perspective and begins to act in new ways. Transformation may or may not occur at this juncture, depending on the willingness and readiness of key members of the organization. Transformative change is a fundamental shift in perceptions, values, and consciousness. This kind of change involves a profound transmutation of the prevailing vision of reality. New meaning for the organization is established, which completely alters its basic ways of responding to its environment.

OT versus OD

Many authors have attempted to explain Organization Transformation by comparing and contrasting it with Organization Development (OD). For instance, Ackerman (1986) compares transformational change with developmental change. She states that transformational change is more traumatic and profound than developmental or transitional change. In essence, transformational change is somewhat out of the organization's direct control, and it produces future states that are largely unknown until they evolve. Like other authors, Ackerman maintains that transformational change occurs when an organization falls prey to demands from the environment. In other words.

The organization reacts, contorts, and struggles against these pressures until a break-down occurs, often destroying the organization as it was known. However, from the remains of the old emerges a new form, equipped to handle more sophisticated demands. (p. 68)

John Adams (1984) also discusses differences between OT and OD. OD, reflecting its academic roots, is based primarily on behavioral science theories and the collection and analysis of organization data. OT does not reject theory, but shifts the primary focus from theory to the creation of humanistically oriented visions for organizations. It is important to note, however, that OT and OD do not represent an either/or polarity; each is very useful within particular contexts: OD offers important technologies for helping an organization or a unit within an organization operate effectively within the parameters of its stated mission and goals. On the other hand, OT technologies are designed to help an organization explore its very purpose and fundamentally realign itself with its environment. Where OD focuses on issues of effectiveness within a given purpose, OT focuses on changing the purpose itself.

Johnston (1987) also distinguishes between Organization Transformation concepts and Organization Development concepts. For him, transformation involves a completely new context and configuration of behaviors, roles, attitudes, motives, beliefs, and values; while development involves the unfolding, refining, and strengthening of behaviors, roles, attitudes, motives, beliefs, and values. Johnston emphasizes that Organization Transformation and Organization Development ideally work together as follows:

An analogy illustrating how transformation and development work together is that of a baby who has been transporting him or herself solely on all fours, now rather suddenly stands holding on to a chair, and takes a wobbly step or two. This change we can call . . . "transformation" for the reason that the context, content, and processes of experience appears to the child as a major shift from a "crawling context" to an "upright and waking context." If the baby is to become an expert walker, even runner, his or her psycho-muscular coordination must be strengthened and refined. Such "developmental" processes usually require a considerable length of time. (p. 15)

It is evident from the literature that OD has its roots in behaviorist concepts; that is, an underlying assumption of OD is that a change in attitude starts with a change in behavior. OT, on the other hand, is premised on the perspective that an attitude change starts with expanding one's conscious awareness of different possible options. Then one selects new options and envisions their fulfillment.

Kilmann and Covin (1988) state that OD and OT are completely different phenomena. If they were not different, Kilmann and Covin argue, there would be little justification for adding OT to the already jargon-filled social and behavioral sciences. There is a general consensus among some researchers that OT is qualitatively different from OD. Tables in the Appendices adapted by Fletcher (1988) from Levy and Merry illustrate several essential differences. In summary, the tables show that OD primarily uses traditional problem-solving strategies that involve a step-by-step process, while OT looks for symbolic patterns that lend meaning to behavior. Again, it is important to think of OT and OD as complementary strategies, not mutually exclusive approaches to organization change.

OT INTERVENTIONS

Our final exploration is in the area of Organization Transformation interventions. There are various processes, methods, techniques and strategies developed by OT practitioners and theorists to facilitate the transformation of organizations. Most of the literature explored thus far has been concerned with explaining what OT is, or is not. Equally relevant are explanations of how OT works and the broad variety of activities and interventions involved.

Buckley and Perkins (1985) describe the processes of Organization Transformation as being similar to death and rebirth. They outline a seven-stage process that identifies the dynamics of transformative change:

1. *Unconsciousness Stage*: Organization transition begins gradually with a period of organization unconsciousness that builds a readiness for change.
2. *Awakening Stage*: The developing awareness and surfacing symptoms form a message to all involved of needed change.
3. *Reordering Stage*: Reordering is a probing process integrating the new catalyst with the existing situation and beginning to challenge underlying assumptions of the past.
4. *Translation Stage*: Translation is the process of integrating information, metaphorical images and personal visions of the unconsciousness, awakening and reordering stages.
5. *Commitment Stage*: Commitment is when the organization takes responsibility for implementation of the new vision.
6. *Embodiment Stage*: In embodiment, leadership and employees work together to bring the transformed vision into day-to-day operations.

7. *Integration Stage*: As the embodiment of the desired change becomes widespread, the organization reaches a stage of integration. (Buckley and Perkins 1985, pp. 48–49)

Movement through all seven cycles is necessary for fully integrated transformative change. Seldom do organizations move smoothly or linearly through these stages. And the tempo at which they move varies as they jump backward and forward in a seemingly random manner. This process is not like traditional linear mechanistic concepts, which are concerned with an orderly supplying of something that is missing or fixing something defective. Instead, it is a cyclical process of "disintegration" and "reformation."

Similarly, Gemmill and Smith (1985) write that transformative change within a system follows four basic processes:

1. *Disequilibrium Conditions*: The assumed condition within which change becomes possible is one of turbulence, environmental, and/or internal.
2. *Symmetry Breaking*: This implies that the system is somehow breaking down its usual processes.
3. *Experimentation*: Through the experimentation process, the system create new possible configurations around which it can eventually reformulate.
4. *Reformulation Processes*: In this formative process, new configurations are tested within the new environmental constraints and with respect to the system's previous level of development. For this to take place, the system must be highly resonant, both internally and externally, to both its subsystem alignments and its alignments with the contingencies of the environment. (pp. 758–759)

Levy and Merry (1986) propose the following four developmental stages as representative of the process of transformation in organizations:

1. Crisis
2. Transformation
3. Transition
4. Stabilization and development (p. 273)

Levy and Merry's fourth stage, "stabilization and development," like Buckley and Perkins' "integration stage," recognizes the need for the institutionalization of the transformation. Transformation in and of itself is not enough; stabilization and development are critical to the process. In an even more elaborate schema, Johnston (1987) describes OT as consist-

ing of both transformational and developmental phases in which psycho-
organic and problem-solving processes are merged:

Organization Transformation Phase:
- Current paradigm
- Stimulus (self-generated or environment-generated)
- Unfreezing from old paradigm (context, task, content, and process)
- Discovery/creation/innovation of new paradigm
- Refreezing in new paradigm
- Implementation of new content via new processes
- Feedback (confirmation or disconfirmation, i.e., detection of problems[s])

Organization Development Phase:
- Identification of problem(s)
- Setting problem priorities
- Developing and sharing of data
- Joint-action planning
- Implementation and testing of selected alternatives
- Performance review (feedback) and further refining and strengthening action. (Johnston, unnumbered manuscript, 1987)

Creating a new vision of possibilities for a new organization appears to be the starting point for many OT interventions. For example, Moore and Gergen (1988) write that a new vision is the starting point for Organization Transformation interventions, and that it is then necessary to mobilize the energy needed to achieve the new vision. Taking a slightly different approach from many of the other writers, Finney, et al. (1988) goes as far as to suggest that each new vision should be a blueprint of how the organization will appear after its transformation. Using an approach similar to Finney, et al., de Bivort (1984) states that transformation suggests a highly positivist, vision- and action-oriented strategy, in which activist visionaries, or what they call "evolutionary managers," deliberately transform an organization using high-level skills, models, methods, and techniques.

Each of these models, methods, and techniques is based on theories that may or may not be appropriate for an organization given its particular stage of development, structure, market, or other environmental variables. Thus, it is prudent to take a contingency approach to OT interventions, and remember that OT practitioners need to be eclectic—flexibly using a repertoire of approaches, techniques, and models. With so many options available, it is important to realize that there is no one best way to facilitate change or transformation in organizations. Viewing the past gives only a distorted perspective of a drastically different future. Therefore, organizational leaders must learn to depend on a creative balance of old, new, and cutting-edge concepts and techniques.

RESEARCH DESIGN

The first question for the study was: "Who are these Organization Transformation theorists and practitioners?" It would be necessary to take in the whole gestalt (including history and significant experiences) of each person in order to derive a comprehensive answer to the question. Since such a large-scale undertaking would not be practical, perhaps the next best approach is the in-depth interview method used in this study.

The in-depth interview method is holistic. It involves looking closely at the phenomenon and trying to understand what is going on. It also avoids the mistake of researching a "pocket." Thus, this study looked for the broad patterns and issues that gave meaning to the participants.

Pilot Interviews

The first interview, with Robert W. Johnston, was used as a pilot to test the questions in the initial Interview Guide. That interview provided valuable information about the clarity and sequencing of the questions. The Guide was revised to reflect that information. Because Johnston is a significant contributor to the theoretical literature of Organization Transformation, a follow-up interview was conducted with him which sought more information based on the changes in the Interview Guide. In addition, an interview was conducted with a professional consultant, Evangelina Holvino, who clearly did not identify herself as an OT Consultant. The purpose of that interview was, again, to test the questions. No changes were made to the Guide as a result of the interview with Holvino and data accumulated from it were not used in the study.

A Contrasting Point of View

It was discovered during the interview with Michael Burkart, that he, also, did not identify with Organization Transformation, although he had some knowledge of the area. Because the sole purpose of this study is to focus on OT practitioners and theorists, the data collected from that interview were not used.

Selection of Participants

The entire field of Organization Transformation theorists and practitioners was originally estimated to be very small. The plan to approach potential participants for this study was, therefore, critical and designed to maximize the sample size. Participants for the study were selected so as to ensure the inclusion of as many theorists and practitioners of OT as was possible and practical, given the small total population, time and monetary constraints. Although the numbers of theorists and practitioners initially appeared to be very small, this investigator has since gained a better appreciation for the growing numbers of people involved in the phenomenon of OT. The following procedure was used to assure the largest possible number of participants.

- Because participants were most successfully located through informal channels, the investigator started with two practitioners and theorists of OT already known to her (Dr. Norma Jean Anderson, and Dr. Robert W. Johnston). Personal referrals and introductions to others in the area of OT were requested. An identical request was then made of each succeeding person who agreed to be interviewed.

- In addition, a meeting of the Organization Transformation Network (OTN), located in the Boston area, was attended—which provided other participants.

- The OT Network in the Washington D.C. area was also contacted. Mr. Harrison Owen and Dr. John Adams, who are two of the founders of the national and international OT symposiums and coiners of the phrase "Organization Transformation," were interviewed.

A contingency plan to access participants should the informal process fail was not used. As the data collection process proceeded, it became clear that there would be no problem finding participants through informal channels. In fact, the investigator was compelled to limit the sample due to the large volume of data collected.

Based on the literature search and initial interviews, it was originally estimated that the "universe" of OT theorists and practitioners totaled approximately twenty-five people. That proved to be a very significant underestimation of the people who are both overtly and covertly practicing and theorizing about OT. A revised conservative estimate would be well over 2,000.

The Interview Guide

The in-depth interviews were characterized by open-ended, free re-sponse questions designed to encourage the participant to reveal her/his thoughts, feelings, interpretations, and sense of meanings. The interviews were, for the most part, informally conversational. The flexible interview structure is outlined on the Interview Guide shown in the Appendices. The Interview Guide acted as a cueing system to assure that certain topics were covered. The framing questions, which were derived from the gaps in the literature, are reflected in the Interview Guide.

Interview Process

Each interview lasted between one and three hours, and was audio-recorded. There were only two follow-up interviews required to obtain additional data. One of them was due to tape recorder malfunction (inter-view with Donald Carew), and the other was added to obtain more information from the pilot interview (with Robert Johnston).

The conversation flow was allowed to influence the sequencing of the questions, and follow-up questions not shown on the Guide were freely asked to explore and better understand participants' meanings and definitions of concepts. Participants were asked most, or all, of the questions shown on the Guide. All participants were given the opportunity to review their tape recordings and interview transcripts to assure that the raw data reflected their backgrounds and their understandings of the phenomenon of OT.

The process of analyzing and interpreting the large volumes of raw data required skill, insight, and lots of patience. According to several experts in the field of qualitative data analysis (Miles and Huberman, 1984; Patton, 1980; Spradley, 1979; and Taylor and Bogdan, 1984), developing a conceptual framework of schema to organize the large amounts of data generated by qualitative inquiry is a necessary and crucial step to under-standing. Because the questions on the Interview Guide reflected the framing questions for the study, the Guide itself was used as the primary conceptual framework for the data. By dividing the twenty-two Interview Guide questions into seven separate categories, the process of reducing, organizing, analyzing and attaching meaning to the data was aided. The seven sections of the Interview Guide are as follows:

1. Meanings
2. Background

3. OT vs OD
4. OT'ers
5. Personal Philosophy
6. Consequences/Applicability
7. Case

Profiles

Profiles of the participants that appear in Chapter 2 were developed from the second section of the Interview Guide, "Background." The two questions in the "Background" section have to do with participants' personal backgrounds in Organization Transformation. The questions asked are: (1) How did you come to be interested in OT? And, (2) Where has this interest in OT led you?

The profiles were developed by first identifying the *complete* response that each participant made to each question. Profiles include responses to follow-up questions asked by the researcher, which were designed to obtain more information than participants gave in their initial responses. And the profiles include answers to questions seeking definitions to words and phrases that participants used in their initial or follow-up responses. Once the complete responses were identified and separated from the rest of the raw data, the profiles were edited for grammar, sentence structure, and to eliminate repetitions. Questions asked by the interviewer are not shown in the profiles. Although profiles were edited, diligent care was taken to leave the responses, to as great extent as possible, in the words of the participants. Interviewer observations, transcripts, and documents provided by participants were used to compose the brief biographical sketches shown at the beginning of each profile.

Ten men and four women participated in this study. A breakdown of participants by race and gender follows:

- 1 Black female
- 2 Black males
- 3 white females
- 8 white males

Of the fourteen participants, nine have doctoral degrees; four are currently university professors; all but one are consultants; ten own or co-founded their own consulting firms; and all but two are published authors, as shown

Table 1.1
A Comparative Chart of Participant Age, Degree, Occupation, and Publications

	Age	Highest Degree	Univ. Prof.	Consulting C=Consultant IC=Internal Consultant O=Owner or Founder	Publications
Adams	46	Ph.D.		O	43
Anderson	57	Ed.D.	X	O	9
Bartunek	44	Ph.D.	X		35
Carew	54	Ed.D.	X	O	27
Esty	54	Ph.D.		O	7
Gordon	40	M.Ed.		IC	0
Ingle	41	Ph.D.		IC	12
Johnston	59	Ph.D.		O	28
Kueppers	44	M.A.		O	0
Owen	53	M.A.		O	3
Rollins	51	B.A.		O	5
Shandler	42	Ed.D.		O	10
Simmons	50	Ph.D.	X	O	56
Stetson-K.	40	M.Ed.		C	1

in Table 1.1. The number of publications shown in this table represent a very rough estimate based on documents supplied by participants.

SUMMARY

In conclusion, the literature shows that Organization Transformation generally happens when the organization's environment drastically changes and the old ways of doing business are no longer possible, and a new way becomes essential—the alternative being extinction. Transformation occurs when unexpected forces in the environment converge upon the organization and exert tremendous pressures for change. Organizations can attempt to change by doing a better job of implementing the paradigm they have been using (i.e., first-order change) or they can choose a new paradigm (i.e., Organization Transformation). Most organizations select the first approach, which results in marginal changes. The turbulent, fast-paced environments that characterize our post-modern world have proven that marginal, incremental changes in organizational practices are inadequate for survival in the global marketplace.

The current state of the art in OT may be summarily described as ecological, holistic, humanistic approaches to radical, revolutionary, second-order change in the entire context of an organization's system. OT involves transformative changes in the fundamental nature of the organization in relation to its ecosystem, and requires completely new ways of thinking, behaving, and perceiving by members of the organization. OT strategies can help an organization to be more flexible and responsive to internal and external environments. Also, OT strategies tend to intensify the organization's social consciousness and accordingly transform its vision and mission.

Transformation is profound, traumatic, and painful. However, when the process is carried to its completion, the results may be compared to that of giving birth. A new organizational life-form emerges that marks the death of the old way of being. Transformation often produces a future state that is largely unknown until it evolves. However, the new form that emerges from the remains of the old organization is usually better equipped to handle the new environmental demands.

Today, many organizations are struggling with transformational changes. These include transportation, communications, and metal-processing organizations, among others. If the transformation is successful, the organization becomes something entirely different in context, structure, content and process. Indeed, Organization Transformation occurs not only in the structure and behavior, but also in the consciousness of an orgnaization. The essence of transformation lies in the new mind and spirit of the organization as it moves from one form to another in continuous transformation—from state A to state B, to states C, D, E, and so on.

Gaps in the Literature

What the literature up to this time does not reveal is specific information about Organization Transformation theorists and practitioners—who are they? What are their underlying philosophical assumptions? What do they have in common that makes them an identifiable group of theorists and practitioners? On what points do they differ? What do they think are the important contributions of OT? What impact do they predict that OT will have on organizations? Using data from the study described in this chapter, the remainder of this book attempts to provide answers to those questions.

2

Profiles of Organization Transformation Theorists and Practitioners

The purpose of this chapter is to give the reader a "sense" of the people who are practicing and theorizing about Organization Transformation. The chapter contains short sketches drawn from the words of the fourteen professionals who participated in this study.

All of the participants are active in their professions. Each of them is involved in a variety of activities such as writing, teaching or lecturing, consulting, with responsibilities in professional and other organizations. Each person's story constitutes his or her unique response to the following two questions: How did you come to be interested in OT? And, where has this interest led you?

PROFILE: JOHN ADAMS

White male, age 46
Director and Co-Founder of Eartheart Enterprises, Inc.
Ph.D., Organization Behavior
Case-Western Reserve University

My own personal interest in OT started in the mid- to late 1970s when I was developing a lot of research, training and consulting in the area of stress management. I was studying and taking post-doctoral courses in nutrition and physiology and endocrinology to add to my Organization Development background so that I could present the stress and health area from a very wide spectrum. As a part of those studies, I started studing the mind and how we create our own stress. I began studying cognitive psychology, and at the same time began studying with a Sufi leader in this country named Piervalat Kahn. Actually, it was interesting how I was lead to him. I was lead to Karl Pribram who has a holographic theory of how the mind operates through the cognitive side. Karl Pribram was giving a weekend seminar up in New York state, so I went to the seminar not knowing anything really about the sponsoring organization, which was called Omega Institute. It was their second year. What it turned out to be was a weekend dialogue between Karl Pribram and Piervalat Kahn, and while I enjoyed what Karl Pribram was saying, and it was reinforcing what I had read about him, Piervalet blew my mind with the things he was saying.

For the next several years, I would go back every summer to Piervalat's community to a retreat and follow that with ten days at Omega doing a weekend and a five-day intensive. So that really began opening up a lot of new avenues both from the cognitive end and the spiritual side of things for me, which I began using in my work in organizations more and more. I became less concerned with teaching meditation and less concerned about our birth rights as co-creators and things like that. I became more value- and integrity-oriented in my own work in terms of what I was suggesting that people would have to do if they're going to live well and perform well in a healthy organization.

So one summer at Omega, a Thursday evening, there was an opportunity for anybody who was there as a participant to teach. Participants could put out their sign and anybody that wanted to would come—they did that every summer. I think it was the summer of 1982 that I gave a talk to a dozen or so people who showed up on how I work with what I called, for their benefit, "new-age principles" and working with health and stress in organizations. These were people coming from food co-ops, street clinics, etc. They were amazed that I was doing these kinds of things with the Exxons and the Duponts of the world—because they didn't really believe that that was possible.

We started playing around with what to call it. I didn't really have a name for it. It was stress management, it was OD. We'd been talking about transformation at Omega, and I said "I guess it's transformation of organizations," as we'd been talking about individual transformation; that was the theme of the week and they could relate to that. Well, I came back to Washington and I started using that language, and somebody said "Oh, if that's what you're thinking you ought to meet Harrison Owen, you ought to talk to Frank Burns because I've just heard them using the same language recently"—an example of synchronicity in 1982. Harrison was using the terminology in his work with myth and organizations; Ackerman was using it in terms of her work with transition, energy, and flow; and Frank Burns was using it in terms of his NLP background and working with creativity in organizations and high performance. So we all got together. We started putting the first conference together, and the next summer in 1983 we had this gathering in New Hampshire.

I had become intrigued by the synchronicity we'd experienced, so I started asking around and I found a lot of people thinking in the same ways, so I invited people to write papers for a book, which has been a real successful little book, *Transforming Work*. It has never been marketed, nor has it ever been distributed at bookstores. It has done really well, word of mouth. It has kind of captured the moment, I guess, with synchronicity and the coming together of these ideas. And when you really look into it, it's not new stuff. Bob Tannenbaum was writing about the same stuff back in the 1960s before "Organization Development" had even been coined. So it's not "revolutionary" new. But that's how I moved into it—by coining a phrase to try to communicate with some people who were of a different perspective than most of the people I was accustomed to, and finding other people who were speaking the same language simultaneously.

I just returned from India. I conducted a month-long seminar series with Sabina Spencer there. We did five seminars called Strategic Leadership, which are about our most leading-edge ideas of the moment in terms of vision and higher purpose and creativity at work, creating a sustainable high-performance environment in times of change, and so on. And we never have had a better reception for our ideas anywhere in the world as in Indian top management. It's great! I have a whole album full of pictures.

We do about 40 percent of our work in Europe. We're flying to London tomorrow night after ten days at home for Sabina. I have a couple of clients in England. Sabina will be going on to Brussels to work with a multinational organization, and then we'll be working together in Amsterdam two weeks from right now—a program called Transition and Transformation, which is a two-day version of a program that we do for National Training

Laboratories (NTL). Our partnership sort of evolved in November of 1984 shortly after this OT movement started. We've been together since August of 1985, and we like to work together as much as possible. We started out saying we wanted to be together 50/50, work together, and work separately, but now we're saying we want to work together more than that, so we do. Our styles are so complementary and additive, synergistic I guess. People get a lot more from us when we're together than they get from either of us separately. We do magic together. We talk about our work sometimes as sowing butterfly seeds, with the idea that what's death to the caterpillar is transformation to the butterfly. So you can choose whether you'll have caterpillar consciousness or butterfly consciousness. Anyway, so where it's led is that our partnership has really evolved out of just discovering our joint interest.

The leading edge that I'm working on now is what I call automatic pilot work—individual belief systems, which has been my work for five or six years now. In *Transforming Work*, there's a chapter on beliefs and performance and well-being. I've got another paper from last summer which involves some of that. I'm not quite sure how to do this yet, but I want to tie that in with purpose. I've got a book that I want to write called *Working on Purpose*, double entendre, just like all the others; for example: are you transforming work or are you doing the work of transformation? Everything I think of has double meanings, like *Transforming Work* and *Transforming Leadership*.

PROFILE: NORMA JEAN ANDERSON

Black female, age 57
Professor of Education/Organization Development
University of Massachusetts
Ed.D., Educational Psychology
University of Illinois

I remember reading something about OT—I don't think I created the term! I don't even remember what I read. But then, I said, "Ahah! This is really where we need to be!" Because it was so in tune with my whole idea about people needing to be transformed. A slogan on our church bulletin talks about being transformed by the renewing of our minds. What it is saying is that we are about teaching and enlightenment. We are about instruction, and I think that an organization that is about enlightenment and instruction, is about training, keeping people abreast, keeping people in tune with the world, being on the cutting edge. It's about people being in a position where other systems will say, "This organization is effective, it's making a difference, the people are empowered, it's not static." I do think there is a time for organizations to be in the same place for awhile; but, as the world develops, organizations should at some point develop and be transformed.

Every now and then organizations should ask, "What business are we in?" And maybe they should transform if they get an answer that calls for transformation. If they answer in a way that does not call for transformation, they should remain where they are and continue to develop. If the answer calls for transformation, then they need to change in order to be in tune with the world, and with the conditions of society. I have been involved most of my life with a lot of change. I'm fifty-seven, so I've lived long enough to go through a lot of changes in society and in life in general. I lived through the sixties, which was about a world of change—it was a very impactful experience to be a Black woman in the 1960s. I was just finishing my doctorate at the time President Kennedy was assassinated. Young people were looking at the world and saying, "Why should we even try to be anybody?" When Dr. Martin Luther King Jr., John Kennedy, and Robert Kennedy were killed, the message to young people seemed to be: "Don't grow up to be anything because you're not going to live to tell it."

School systems also needed change because they were depleted of a lot of talent, teachers were leaving because they were disheartened and low-paid. I lived and worked in St. Paul, Minnesota, in an area where we bussed Black children and white children. There was also a large Jewish population in the community. We all got together and called ourselves Parents for Integrated Education—we were about change. We were about transforming that whole school system into a system that didn't have this little pocket of the poor in one area, or Black in one area, or whatever. So, it was a big change with creative ideas which came from the community.

Then, I joined the University of Massachusetts, School of Education. I was brought in at a time when we had a new dean who decided that he wanted to do something big—the universtiy had given him three years to do anything he wanted to do. He decided to transform the whole School of Education. They had about twenty-seven faculty members when he first came and he hired about thirty new faculty, whom he hand-picked. They were not just education people, they were doctors and lawyers and Peace

Corps directors—people from various backgrounds. That particular mix of people, coming from different perspectives and different points of view, was really transforming. They made UMass School of Education a totally different school! It was no longer made up of just people who had gotten their degrees in Education, Educational Administration, Teaching, or History; in come people who had a variety of backgrounds and a variety of experiences.

When I came here the year after all this started, we decided to admit doctoral candidates. I admitted 700 doctoral students: 350 Blacks, 350 whites, 350 women and 350 men. It was totally different, in terms of what it had been—an exclusive all white system. It was totally different in terms of the background and experience that were brought in by not only faculty, but doctoral students! We had totally different expectations of what education was all about in that we said education is a freeing experience, not a limiting experience. So we decided to let doctoral students and master's students and undergraduates call us by our first names. After working so hard for the title of "Doctor," I lost it when I came here and was just "Norma Jean" again! I learned to live with that—it was freeing, not only for the students, but also for me.

It was freeing when we went out as teams into corporations to consult. The people in those corporations didn't know at first who was "doctor" and who was student because we called each other by first names. It was freeing because we were able to decide our own curriculum. We totally threw out the old curriculum. We decided to teach what we felt students needed and still, to this day, we don't have a bound curriculum—that started in 1970. What was freeing, too, was that we went to individualized instruction, knowing that every individual was unique and special. So, therefore, students needed to have a hand in selecting their own course of study, with the aid of an advisor. They also could choose their own advisors and let their advisors go (fire them) if they wanted to. "Pass-Fail" grades were introduced and that was freeing, also. All the research literature showed that it didn't make a difference in learning whether students were graded or not. The students, of course, sometimes seemed to learn more when they weren't graded—they focused on securing the content of the material as opposed to a grade. So, that was an exciting transforming experience to me.

Another transforming experience that I had was working with the National Training Lab and coming in at a time when people were really looking at themselves and the whole business, which was an "old-boys network." We started asking ourselves: "What is this business anyway? Is it just something we're doing for personal gratification or do we start translating it and carrying our art out into the community, increasing our training programs and organizational consultancy?" Everything that we do now!

I've also been very active in the church. My husband was a minister, and we as a family went about transforming ourselves! When we saw that we weren't what we should be, when we saw that we were too traditional—trying to live by tradition versus what we felt should happen in the here-and-now—we decided to look to ourselves rather than looking at any past patriarchs as a model. Our family was indeed another transforming experience. Our family has really lived a transforming life, knowing who we are, and defining our own selves, and living out of that definition rather than living out of someone else's definition. We have four children—that, too, was an experience of letting go. Often we would say, "Gosh! I'd better tell these children what to do so they won't make so many mistakes, and because I feel that I know better." Whenever we got to that point, I feel we were not helping them to transform, because what we were doing was trying to motivate them from the outside. I think the true transforming power is from within. So, even though you may be the mother or the father or the sister or the brother, you are still outside of that person and that person's transformation comes from within. It's hard to let go—very hard.

So, those experiences manifest in my values. My values manifest in my attitude toward people, the projects I choose to be identified with, the organizations I work for and choose to consult in, my choice of colleagues and peers and friends. They manifest in the church I choose to belong to, the design of the curriculum I use when I do training and, also, they manifest in the way I talk.

PROFILE: JEAN BARTUNEK

White female, age 44
Associate Professor of Organizational Studies
Boston College
Ph.D. in Social and Organizational Psychology
University of Illinois at Chicago

I became interested in OT partly because of joining a religious order in 1966 that then went and changed—gigantically. I wrote a paper that was published in 1984 in *Administrative Science Quarterly*, that described the major transformation in this order. In 1962–66, there was an event in the Catholic church called the Second Vatican Council, that changed the Catholic church immensely. One of the things that came out of it was a directive to religious orders that they had to change in a lot of ways, and that a lot of the momentum for the change had to be participative. That was an especially amazing thing because religious orders were really hierarchical; they made a machine bureaucracy look mild in comparison. I happened to join the order shortly after that. Just before I joined, things started changing a lot, from very traditional practices; for example, to movement away from everybody teaching in Sacred Heart schools, to changing the understanding of the apostolic mission of the order, etc.

The order used to view itself as having a dual orientation, until the Second Vatican Council said, "You can't have two orientations, you have to pick one or the other," so it picked apostolic. As I mentioned, we use to be incredibly hierarchically structured with a million levels of bureaucracy, and that's pretty much gone. Every person in my order in the U.S. essentially now reports to the Provincial, who is one person. Except, obviously, we don't report much. There's much more of a sense of collaboration. The understanding of the vows has changed immensely, like obedience used to be defined as responding to the sound of a bell, and now it's more collaboratively discerning God's will. So virtually everything in their basic understanding has changed since the time I've been in the order. That's probably one of the reasons I became interested in organizational change. It was, without a doubt, a transformational change. Although some people would dispute that it was a change for the better, I think that it was for the better, I prefer it like this. A lot of people have left religious orders. There is a huge decline in the number of people, which some people attribute to this kind of change.

The way I happened to get interested in transformation is related: A few years ago nobody was thinking in transformational terms at all. I wrote a paper for *Administrative Science Quarterly* in which I tried to say that the normal ways of talking about change didn't fit, that the term that made the most sense was second-order change, which is from Watzlawick's book of 1974. Second-order change is a qualitative shift in the ways in which people interpret something, as opposed to just getting better at what they're already doing. As the notion of transformation evolved, it appeared that this notion included second-order change, and that those were sometimes synonymous terms. As a result of my writing that article, I was invited by Bob Quinn to write a chapter for a book that he and Kim Cameron edited,

Paradigms in Transformation. I wrote a kind of theoretical chapter and basically tried to figure out what I think theoretically happens during transformation. A lot of the theory in that article was based on my experiences and also on some other work a friend and I had written about in the tracing of a failed change project in a medium-size food processing plant.

That is how I became involved, by writing and trying to make sense of something that had happened in my life, and by using some categories to explain that, which then got subsumed into transformation. Certainly a lot of the writing that I'm doing is still on this topic in some way. My friend and I are writing a book about the failed "quality of working-life" intervention, and the title of that book is going to be *Creating Alternative Realities at Work.* One of the things we're trying to explore in that book is what consultants might do to foster transformational change, and some of the ways it can get screwed up. Most of the work I've done since 1984 has been much more about ways that transformation doesn't happen than about the ways it does. This semester I'm teaching a class in Organizational Change and Development, and certainly I'll talk about transformation as one of the topics. I'll force people to read some of my stuff, for better or for worse.

In terms of what I do personally: last summer our Order had its first ever national conference and I gave a workshop on transformation as it might apply to our Order. In October I was at a conference sponsored by some religious groups—different leaders of religious orders, and I ended up giving a one-hour talk on Organizational Transformation—which wouldn't have been a big deal except that they'd told us not to come prepared to give any talks at all. But people wanted talks, so I had to sort of extract this from my head. It actually went pretty well. One of the things that came out of it was a couple of days ago I got a letter from one of the sponsoring agencies asking me to write a short article on transformation for the newsletter of this agency. The reason I mentioned that is that one of the things I know from an organizational behavior focus, and also from attribution theory, is that people's normal tendency when something is not going well is to say that individuals are messing up.

Transformation, in my experience, is a real difficult experience. It isn't just something that's real fun, where people say, "Isn't this great that we have all of these different conflicting perspectives." Instead, they say, "I think this is terrible, and nobody knows what's going on anymore and people disagree, and that's terrible." It's real stressful for people. Many different Orders are showing signs of stress that they weren't showing before in the 1950s and 1960s under a super-regimented organized bureaucracy. A lot of people who are religious with sort of a clinical background are defining the signs of stress as, "Look at the terrible personality characteristics of people in religious life—wasn't it awful who we admitted in the 1950s," or something like that. From my perspective the symptoms they're showing are due to the fact that they are going through a stressful and uncertain time, as opposed to just perhaps their personalities.

One of my aims for religious orders is to do what I can to convince people that there is at least a slim possibility that it's not that people have bad personalities, but that these kinds of changes are meaningful in themselves. It's hard to do that—many people just don't operate out of an organizational perspective. So stuff that happens organizationally doesn't compute as an honest-to-goodness cause of something. Especially if they've had some sort of clinical training, what they see is individual problems, without a corresponding sense of how some organizational event could have caused it. So one of my aims, which I know I'm doomed to fail in, but I'm going to try to do it anyway, is to convince at least a couple of religious orders that if people are having difficulty, it isn't just that the people are weird.

When I teach the Organization Development class the assignment for all of the students is to try to change something in an organization; sometimes that doesn't work. When I present the transformation perspective, it sometimes helps them to understand why it didn't work. In other words, to get something changed they would have needed a much more radical change in their frame of reference.

PROFILE: DONALD K. CAREW

White male, age 54

Professor of Organizational Development and Applied Group Studies, University of Massachusetts

Founding Associate, Blanchard Training and Development

Independent Consultant

Ed.D., Counseling Psychology, University of Florida

It started years ago by just being perplexed by the dichotomy between what was said in this society, and what actually happened. This applied to schools, to race relations, to organizations, to different churches, where we espoused an egalitarian philosophy—the dignity of all people. I kept seeing real discrepancies in the way organizations functioned and in the values, and the evolution of this society. So there was sort of a stirring in me. At the time,

I thought of it probably more in terms of democratizing our institutions. The organizations in our democratic society were almost fascist in their approach to people. And so I describe it in terms of democratizing the world of work, but not just the world of work—almost everywhere.

I lived in a small town in Ohio, and there were very few minorities there. There was a young Japanese-American who was my age and we became friends. This was right after the Second World War and I had just moved into this town. I received all kinds of stuff from people that I hadn't even thought much about before. That was an awakening for me. This "awakening" has led me into lots of trouble! I remember in college during the 50s and early 60s, I happened to be in a dorm on a floor where about half the kids were Black, and they were at one end of the floor, and we were at the other end of the floor. This was at Ohio University, where I got my undergraduate degree. I was in my freshman year. Anyway, we became friends and one of the things that I remember was some conversations with these guys about having problems getting haircuts. I never thought about it before, so I decided that I would go to the only Black barbershop in town. After I'd been doing that for awhile, I noticed there were never any Blacks in there, and I asked the barber about it, and he said he wouldn't cut Blacks' hair because it would be bad for his business. Well, I learned to cut Black men's hair. Also, there was this greasy-spoon restaurant that I discovered wouldn't serve Blacks, so I got involved in some boycotting. I was also a member of a fraternity that wouldn't let anybody in who wasn't WASPish. The group there—the majority of them—wanted to do something about it, but the national order wouldn't budge, so I resigned. So these kinds of experiences led me into contact with other people with similar concerns.

Those different connections with different people who had different kinds of views were what led me in the direction of Organization Transformation—they challenged my thinking. Right after high school I did some traveling for about a year. I wanted some life experience before I jumped into college. I spent some time working with itinerant workers. There was another example for me of the great differences—so all those kinds of impactful experiences led me to wanting change—it was like a drive in that direction. This drive has manifested in my consulting and my teaching—I see it in all that I do. From my perspective, I see it in the Group Dynamics courses that I teach. Its one of the reasons I'm committed to National Training Laboratories (NTL), an organization that is trying to live by a more egalitarian style. NTL is one of those transformative organizations.

A lot of the change focus in the 50s and 60s was around race; however, transformation has been a consistent pattern—not just around racial stuff, but around other organizational changes that involved broadening opportunities. I see the whole framework of a T-group as really trying to figure out how to create a way for everybody to be able to grow and to contribute, to be appreciated—no matter what their background or status in life. I see all of the other consulting things that I do as trying to move in that direction—sometimes not as directly. I don't always do things that would fit into the framework of transforming organizations, but whenever I have an opportunity that's the kind of thing I'm trying to influence. When I do training in organizations I come in at a different angle, but always within that transforming frame of reference. By first looking at my own values, I try to help people to see a need for valuing differences and I try to help people to grow.

PROFILE: KATHARINE ESTY

White female, age 54

A Founder and Executive Vice-President of Ibis
Consulting Group, Inc.

Ph.D., Social Psychology, Boston University

I started out working in mental health. I was always interested in the psychology of adults and personal transformation, and so I did a lot of therapy. At the same time I was also doing work with NTL, which was adult education; teaching adults how to learn, seeing adult life as lifelong learning, lifelong education. I became very interested in my NTL work in groups and I started a group therapy program for my Health Center. I was interested in the dynamics of groups in terms of such issues as how to get a group working well, what is an effective work group, and what is an effective therapy group. Then I just took it to the next level of complexity: one of the metaphors I use to explain it is that it's like playing three-dimensional tic tac toe, where an individual is one level, and then you get into two dimensions, but it's really the third dimension of organizations being groups of groups, and then needing some connecting systems that integrate all these groups of working systems. I became interested in transformation, since as a manager I had been in that process myself.

When I was at the Mental Health Center doing group therapy, I was also running an out-patient department with seven clinics and programs in it.

For a while each of those seven directors were reporting to me, and I found myself thinking about the issues of how to transform an organization and how systems fit together. So it was my own experience that gave me the initial impetus. Then I went back to school, but the impetus came from my own experience.

I do not identify myself as an OT practitioner; I say that I'm an Organization Development person. I am, however, interested in transforming organizations. There's an organization in Boston called the OT Network and I occasionally go to a meeting—maybe once every year. There was also an OTN Conference that I went to up in Durham about five years ago and I am interested in those ideas.

Now the book by Kilman and Covin, *Corporate Transformation . . .*, for which I wrote a chapter, is much more of a conservative swing. It contains the writings of people who are interested in organizational change and they are more the academic mainstream OD types. I don't identify myself with the academic part, but I do with mainstream. I have a few concerns about some OT people, at least the ones that are much more into the spiritual thing. I don't think that this group of people should limit the definition of Organization Transformation. I think it's important when you discuss OT to be clear about whether you're talking about that group of people or discussing a process of transforming organizations. It's the second one that I see myself as giving room to.

I'm really trying to transform systems. A lot of people are trainers, and have a program in assertiveness training, or a training program in management development, or a training program in management diversity. But, if you look at the focal point of change, they are trying to change individuals. I would say that my work is much more about systemic change or structural change. I'm going for fundamental change, not trying to change the people necessarily. I know you have to do some training, certainly, and that's part of what I do, but I think that organizational change only comes when you really work on changing the system. So that's what I do.

The arena I'm working in often involves more traditional organizations. I've worked for a lot of smokestack organizations and there are limits to what you can introduce and get paid for. So, while I'm interested in exploring a much more far-out vision of what an organization could be, I tend to be working with more modest goals like managing diversity, or more equity.

I think that my interest in OT has shaped what I try to do with my clients. If I get asked to do a specific job, I try to broaden it out to be for long-lasting change, which means I look at the system. For example, I was asked by the Social Service department of a large teaching hospital to provide a little management development training because their managers weren't interested in managing. Well, instead of taking that piece of work at face value, I worked up front a long time with the director to try to suggest that maybe we should take a look at doing an assessment of the organization, and find out what kind of systems were working and what weren't. And I actually sold that, so what we ended up doing was running some focus groups and developing a steering committee. We used the same model that I wrote about in the Kilmann and Covin book, which included gathering information about the organization, feeding it back to an internal group that was a diagonal slice of the organization—people of all different levels—and using that process of giving them feedback on what they were doing as part of the intervention. The next phase is then to have them plan for changes. The changes are actually at the system level, although they're small changes. They start the ball rolling and begin the process of radical change. That's an example of how I tend to work. I'm interested in organizational change. I take a sturctural approach to change. A lot of things that OD people are interested in, I'm interested in; I'm interested in assessment, I'm interested in collaboration, I'm interested in organizational change, I'm interested in the people side of things, although I use other words to describe those things. In some places, Organization Development is not looked on with favor and I find that it sounds a little weak. What our organization tries to get across is the idea that we are effective and very much part of the business end of things—that we are paying attention to the strategic ends of the company. OT, I think, sounds even more far-out, certainly when you use that term with clients. Although, I might find myself going to a program that was sponsored by the OTN; in that way I would align myself with it.

PROFILE: ALLEN GORDON

Black male, age 40
Internal Consultant to the National Executive Council
Papua, New Guinea
M.Ed., Organization Development
University of Massachusetts

I became interested in OT back in maybe 1975. I did some work with North Carolina's Institute of Behavior with Don Carew, Norma Jean Anderson, Rhonda Gordon, and Carlos Anderson. We were doing something on the use of spirituality in organizations, which is really what transformation is about for me. I also believe that in many ways transformation has to ooccur at the individual level. It has to start within the individual and then it goes out—it's an "in-outward" thing, and not an "outward-inward" thing. I have had experiences where there are moments when things are just flowing effortlessly—where I get a maximum amount accomplished with what seems to be a minimum amount of effort. The focus is not on the effort, but nonetheless great things are being produced. I guess it's mainly a function of my experiences, because I've had most of them within a spiritual realm, or with people who are really into spirituality. When we were doing things together it seemed to just flow.

If it can happen in those situations, I believe it can happen in organizations. I believe that these things are generally transferable because we're talking about a common denominator of people. However, I think that organizations have a lot more things that prevent natural transformation from happening. I think there are a lot of restrictions, etc., that if lifted or viewed in a different way, might allow organizations to transform. In my opinion bureaucracies are the most difficult institutions in which to bring about transformation. They are so rigid with their red tape, rules, procedures, and regulations which are opposed to what is needed for transformation (i.e., creativity, loosening up and allowing things to flow, the use of intuition). In fact, that's true with the work we're doing in Papua, New Guinea. Transformation is like a partner to reform, because when we talk about reform, we're talking about the attitude of transformation. It's not something that you do as a one-shot thing. It's an ongoing process, and as an ongoing process, it's a revitalization, a renewing thing that goes on. Therefore, reform is not a static state. The same is true of transformation—it's a process. When it is operating within an organization people are not bogged down in any of the rules and regulations, although they may exist. The word reform, in the sense that I'm using it, is very radical. I'm talking about it more in the sense of transformation or revolution. To me it's very radical because, by my definition, it gets to the root. We're not looking at the symptoms, but we're now down at the causal level. We're really looking at cleaning up the cause in order to free and release that certain energy that is necessary to get things done with a minimum of effort, and produce tremendous results.

We've been addressing the attitude issue within our organizations in Papua, New Guinea, because people are really fixed in their attitudes. We're talking about shifts—making fundamental shifts in the way people think, which frees up energy to do things. We've been addressing that issue, and that's transformation. We haven't called it that, but, in the same sense we've done a lot of things that we haven't named in the classical sense of what is going on—there hasn't been any need to do that. Intuitively, I believe we called upon a lot of the conceptual frameworks and theories of organization, but we didn't consciously bring in the vocabulary and the nomenclature because it serves no purpose in the implementation of what we're trying to do with people.

We've done a lot of creative work in the sense that our whole approach to this has not been one of imposition or laying on, but of working with people and bringing things out. And so we first bring out the people's views of the problems as they're real to them in the everyday work situations. We explore with them their attitudes in relation to those problems—how they contribute to them, and affect their own work. Also we look at that in terms of their colleagues in other areas—how those relationships might be affected. It's easier for them to see how the attitudes and certain behaviors of their colleagues in other departments affect their work than it is for them to see how their work might affect others—obviously it's easier to see other people's faults. So, we've been approaching it in a way that we've been creating ownership of the problems and, consequently, the solutions are emerging. We even have a system now with diagrams. When we started out, we said, "This is basically what it looks like, where things are with the government now, and what it's intended to do—so let's put that aside—let's start with you." We said we'd come back to it, so we put it aside in order to recreate, if you will, their situation, the issues, and their attitudes. Then we began to look at how our experience in working with other clients fit. So we now have six models that have to do with this Resource Management System. There are three main areas that we're looking at: one area is what I call development planning—it's a new concept for them. They haven't been development planning and without it there's no real sense of direction, nor a way to establish direction—so that's the first thing we needed to do. The next area has to do with budgeting basically—obviously budgeting should fit what you're planning, but their current system is "budget driven." In other words, they figure out what their budget is and then they base the planning on it. And so we're looking at program budgeting as another concept that seems to make sense. Finally, we're looking at the implications of personal management, human resources, and so forth. Finances, as well, are mobilized in order to address the kind of needs that they really consider to be their priorities.

To recreate is to take someone back through an experience they already had or something that they've already done—but from a different view—

to recreate it with a different purpose in mind. When you recreate an experience, it's because you want to bring something forth out of that—something new—which is either to raise your awareness, or your knowledge. But, at least you have ownership because it's not an imposition from the outside. You're bringing something that's from within, out. I call that transformational.

The "we" that I use in discussing all of this is also descriptive of transformation. I think what's important in transformation is that the facilitators also must be transformed in the process of transformation. I think that's one of the principles of transformation. By that I mean that we are constantly working on our own transformation. Another constant that I have brought from my experience is what I call parallel processes. Those who are doing the initiating, mainly the change agents, will face, inevitably, the same kinds of issues and concerns in organizing themselves or preparing themselves to intervene with the client, that the client will face. At each step, as they are intervening with the client, there will be certain issues and concerns that come up with the client, which will come up first with the change agent. And so you have to be involved with your own, in a sense, metamorphosis or transformation in order to be able to effect a transformation of the client—so it's a constant struggle. It's one of the biggest battles I think for us—trying to keep ourselves a team. I don't really think that we've really become that, but I think also that the use of language helps. You have to start the process by saying it—by having a vision of where you want things to be and calling it that. It's like the concept of faith—it is calling it which brings it into reality. So, you say it and people will begin to think that way, energies begin to focus that way, and there's much more of a sense of people operating as a cohesive unit, even though they may not be there yet in reality. So I feel I have a vision of that. I have this vision and commitment that in order for us to be successful with the client, we must first mobilize ourselves into an effective intervention team.

There's a false dichotomy, between personal and professional development, as if they're separate—obviously they're not. I ask, "To what degree do you embrace Organization Transformation? How do you relate this to your personal life?" For me the answer is easy, because, as I said earlier, most of my decisions are made in what I call the spiritual realm. A lot of my decision making is intuitive. That doesn't mean that I ignore realities. For example, If I'd stayed in Papua, New Guinea, I would have probably received a salary increase of one-third. Professionally, it would've made a lot of sense to stay because I would be there to see that project through to completion. I've helped to bring this thing from the embryonic stage to the infant stage to, basically, where it now can walk. The fact that I got along very well with the people was also important to me. There was status working at the very highest levels of government—not that I'm interested in feeding my ego. And in spite of all those reasons to remain in Papua, New Guinea, I'm here, in the United States. I think that it has to do with the spiritual realm; that if I'm going to be integrated and whole, I can't continue to ignore my family. If my life is transforming, I can't ignore certain aspects of it, because I have to be concerned with the whole. That means my decisions also have to be in the spirit as whole. When I brought it up to you earlier, you said "What are you going to do?" and I said "I don't know," it wasn't because I'm fickle and don't know. I simply, but intentionally, don't know; because I know that I'll know when the time is right—I'll know exactly. So, I believe that Organization Transformation is a total commitment, a life-style, and a way to be.

PROFILE: GRANT INGLE

White male, age 41
Acting Director, Office of Human Relations
Universitiy of Massachusetts
Ph.D., Organizational Psychology
University of Massachusetts

I was drawn to the energy flow, seriously. I had a consulting partner, Joan Sneed, who's now in Boston and she got this brochure, she used to work for the Women's Educational Equity Project. Previous to that she was co-director of Everywoman's Center. She looked at this brochure on the First Annual Organization Transformation Symposium. It had these weird colors and stuff, and she said, "I sent it FYI—it looks like it's something for you." And I went, and it was a wonderful experience. I said, "This is my tribe—these are folks I can hang out with." A high percentage of those folks are involved in a computer conference; that's the way we communicate. So it's not only a conference we go to, I could take you in the next room right now and we could ask a question on the computer. It's a very different experience to go to a conference, meet with people and not feel that you've ever left them—you just happen to be seeing them face-to-face in vivid 3-D, as some people say—because afterward you're still interacting with them and seeing how they think all the time by computer. So you continue the really interesting conversation you started with Peter Vaill or Harrison Owen or Frank Byrnes, Lisa Carlson, Sherry Connolly, etc. You go to a conference and you don't really have to say good-bye. I met this group and learned about computer conference and then ended up using the computer conference to stay in touch. So there's a real willingness to try to use technology too, in creative and productive ways. This started in '83 in a conference up at the University of New Hampshire. This is not a group that's in a box. There is a collection of individuals who sort of trail off in really far-out dimensions.

Some of the most positive experiences I've had have been presenting to these folks difficult situations that I've been working on and getting people's reactions, so that's a big part of the activity. I'll give you a really good example. Two and a half years ago in September I helped coordinate a project on this campus called Mass Transformation, in which 4,000 people renovated the library in four days. It was a transformative event involving not just the building. The library is the academic heart of the campus, and it was a disgrace. It needed fixing, the stairwells were loaded with graffiti—it was a mess. We'd just gotten some state money to fix it—to do some structural changes, but it was really still a mess. The big issue was that people didn't care about the building and because they didn't care about it, it got abused. The folks inside didn't feel like they were cared about so they abused the building. And so there was general community agreement that this building was a problem. When a solution was formulated that would use volunteers to basically dress the place up, people liked that approach—so we did it. No one could believe that we'd do something that big and not screw it up—that it would actually come off. And we said: on this day, Sunday the 28th of September at 4:00, the building will be done. Excuse the pun, but it was a very concrete project. At the university, we never have anything that's actually going to be done at a certain time on a certain day. Our building renovations drag on for years. There was an outpouring—a collection of energy, and my job in that whole process was managing the energy. We had to keep things rolling and couldn't let the energy peak too early. We had lots of different groups, faculty, staff, and students, community people, fire fighters, boy scouts, girl scouts, cheerleaders from all the different high schools, alumni, members of the board of trustees—all these different groups with different energy flows and in different cycles—faculty and staff who'd been here for the summer, those just coming back. So it worked. It was an emotional event; a real tear-jerker. A lot of faculty said it was the most positive experience they've ever experienced, and they keep calling those of us who were involved saying, "When are we going to do something like that again? That was great." What did happen, though, was that I went to England, and I still had some real concerns about this project. One of my big learnings about this is that my responsibility to the project should not have ended the day the project was over. I knew we had to manage the energy *afterwards*, and I was real concernerd about that. We had a great closing ceremony. We took a group portrait of 50,000 people. It had the energy of an old '60s demonstration—vibrant—crazy, working, playing and having fun. There was a nice symbolic thing that happened at the end. As the students left the building, we had them sign a mural, and so all the graffiti in the building was moved to this one mural which is in the main lobby right now—it was very powerful. We finished it on September 28. Shortly after that, there were more than eight rebellions on the campus. I don't often reveal this, but I do think the events are connected. I think we raised the energy level of the system. I fault myself and others for not foreseeing, for not doing a better job of thinking through how to manage that energy. I'm not saying there's a one-to-one connection, but you raise the energy level of someone's body, and it has to come out somewhere. I think the events are connected, so my question at the International OT Conference was, are these events connected? Can we do anything about them? Should we do anything about them? If we do this again, what do we need to bear in mind? Is there anything that can be done? That was a very wild session with people from all over the world discussing the questions. Here you are raising positive energy, and is it inevitable that it's going to be balanced out in the system? Is there a calculus, an equilibrium of system energy that's going to be maintained? Can you ever do positive things without negative things popping up? Does doing big positive things increase the probability of big negative things happening? That was a session that was well attended, and people talked for a couple of hours. How can you answer those questions? That's why I say that OT is a group that does mutual exploration.

Where has all of this led me? Well, it's personally helpful in understanding what needs changing and how to make change effective—that's been helpful. OT has also alerted me to a large number of institutional liabilities, mostly in terms of resistance to change. All of a sudden I start asking myself, ok, what are the symbols? What are the myths? We have some really bad performers on the campus. One of the myths is that no one ever gets fired on this campus—it's not true. Another myth: we lack vision, we have no vision, mission or values—in fact the institution is made up of several organizations with different sets of vision and values. OT has given me a way of seeing the university and understanding it in ways that I can articulate and to which other people nod their heads. But in some ways it's also made me pessimistic about the capacity of the institution to make needed changes. Before, I was thinking, "You know, if I could come in with an OD team, a few training programs, new personnel—no problem, we'll get this place fixed up in no time." Then I went into the OT group and they said "You've got to change the myths, rituals and symbols." And I started thinking about faculty—it's largely white and male and tends to remain so—6 percent of full professors are women. It showed me the real enormity of the problem—it wasn't just a matter of making simple changes. So it's been sobering, but also exciting, because we've been able to do things like Mass Transformation, but that is a singular event—it's treated as an abberation. I think it scared the hell out of a lot of folks that that kind of energy level could converge. We now have our administrators talking about being the best in New England—we have the potential to do that here. It's an exciting, vibrant place, but right now we have people running off in a thousand different directions due to the lack of common vision and values. If we could get a little more alignment out of the system we could do that, but we need to make some decisions about what we're going to do. My knowledge about Organization Transformation has made me both optimistic and pessimistic. It's been very helpful to me personally. The whole Civility Week which happened this fall was a modified Harrison Owen open-space design. Create the open space, do some basic directions, invite people to participate. The best idea was from Lori Edmonds, a young Black woman—a graduating senior—who said, "I have this vision—hands across the campus against racism." A line of different people holding hands—stretching clear across the campus. The heaviest of the one hundred events; really the only event of the heart. It was powerful, a very important message. It was not tightly controlled—our office coordinated the event with the help of a lot of people.

OT has changed my model of thinking about how to get things done. Even the name "Mass Transformation" comes right from Organization Transformation. And that was my first real experience in trying to manage a project of that scope and scale in a different way.

PROFILE: ROBERT W. JOHNSTON

White male, age 59
Principal, OmniMind Systems

Counselor; Foundations, Inc.
Ph.D., Management and Organization Development
California Western University

I have been involved with Self and Organization Transformation and Development since 1964. I didn't use that label then. I integrated social change kinds of interventions with technological change—today we call it socio-technical. I was making socio-technical interventions in the latter sixties. In those days I was considered a maverick (probably still am) because OD was oriented solely toward T-groups and interpersonal interventions and that was all that was considered acceptable in the field.

My interest in Self and Organization Transformation and Development started with my being very much disenamored with what was going on in the world and my confusion about who and what I was—my identity. I certainly hadn't found workable answers through conventional organized religion. I'd grown up in a strong Judeo-Christian fundamentalist environment in the Middle West. As I started to question and search I tried many different churches, mystical paths, philosophies, studied comparative religions and even voodoo and witchcraft—all kinds of things—to try to find answers. Still no viable answer. Finally, I started taking up the study of my own dreams, hoping to find the answers within, and that's where I really started to get some answers. I used my dreams for meditation, and I analyzed and synthesized over a ten-year period well over 15,000 of my own dreams. After much winnowing and sifting and what have you, I started to evolve and discovered that my unconscious was really a co-conscious and a presence far beyond anything I had ever imagined before. And I also discovered that when I accepted that co-conscious presence consciously and loved it, my whole set assumptions, beliefs, values, attitudes, and behaviors were transformed—what a different, more positive kind of orientation to life I had. I'm much healthier, more creative, and happier. And so, with that I discovered I was in essence a vital constituent of it—and I could never be separated from it. With that, all the fear of death left me—the fear of bodily death, because I realized that I, as a center of consciousness, would never die. That is, my spirit would never die, only my body would die. Thus, I came to realize that I'm not my body. I have a body, which I love and I take care of, but someday it's going to die, and I, the true psycho-spiritual me, will live on as a part of the living whole—I call it Omniversal Mind-Spirit. That's a very much abbreviated version of what I actually experienced in terms of a radical transformation of my assumptions, beliefs, values, attitudes, and behaviors.

Where has all that led me—I'm principal of a small consulting, education, and research company engaged in Self and Organization Transformation and Development work with all sorts of organizations, including a psychiatric rehabilitation agency whose clients include people with severe thought and feeling disorders. If these transformational concepts and approaches have an acid test, it is in this area of psychosocial rehabilitation. Results thus far have been most encouraging. As to my writing, all twenty-eight of my articles are based on Self and Organization Transformation and Development approaches. I've developed a theoretical base called Integral Psychology; it could be called Integral Organization Change, which is inclusive of Self and Organization Transformation and Development theory and practice. So everything I have done, even though I haven't used in some cases the OT and OD lingo per se, have those concepts and practices built right into them. The most recent one was on the transformative power of dreams, which was published for *Personnel Journal* put out by the American Management Association. It was published last November. Another integral organization change article was "Integrating Spirituality with OD" published in the *Journal of Religion and Applied Behavioral Science* in 1987. I've also custom-written for clients nineteen books and manuals, which again are all based on integral organization change. An example is the *Integral Management Workbook*, accompanied by a book of readings. In addition, I have made seventeen presentations at national and international conferences for such organizations as ODN, the Association for Transpersonal Psychology and the Association for Humanistic Psychology.

As to projects in the works now, I have a number of things—articles, and a book. The book fundamentally is on Self and Organization Transformation and Development. And it's really a compilation of a lot of things I've already published, plus some new things I have not yet published. It's based predominantly on my experience in the field over the last twenty-four years. My experience in Integral Organization Change—Self and Organization Transformation and Development, goes back to 1964. I got my first consulting job in the field at Itek Corporation, in Lexington, Massachusetts, followed by Honeywell, TRW, Black and Decker, McCulloch, Kaiser Permanente, Foundations, and numerous other organizations. I've been in the field ever since as a practitioner, a researcher, adjunct professor in schools of management, and writer.

PROFILE: WILLIAM G. KUEPPERS

White male, age 44
Organization Development and Training Specialist
Private Practice
M.A., Human Development, St. Mary's College

How did I become interested? Well, it's part of a continuum that you might want to isolate out, because, "where's birth"? And I don't mean to be eluding the answer or the question. So, where does it all begin? Some of what I've been thinking about the connectedness of work and spirituality started when I was in grade school. Even then I was thinking in spiritual terms, and becoming aware of my ultimate interconnectedness with the Divine—it goes way back. So there's that seed, that consciousness rather, but nevertheless, it was there; not fully developed, but certainly there. When I was eighteen I was in a religious order of the Catholic church—a thing called the Christian Brothers. You may have heard of Christian Brothers wines and brandies; but, anyway, it was an order devoted to teaching. I was only there for four months; but part of what I learned there was that I don't need to be in a religious setting to be really spiritual—holy. I looked at my father who is a lawyer, I looked at my uncle who ran a very large business—a multimillion dollar business. They were among the most spiritual, quote, "holy" men that I knew. My uncle did wonderful things with people in his organization. He was a big influence on me and provided a model of how you can run a business. They were unionized and yet not unionized; there was never a strike when he was president. He headed one of the first organizations to develop programs for employees. Things like profit-sharing back in the early fifties with employees was new stuff. He also got involved in helping ex-convicts and people who never held jobs before—the continually unemployed, and he worked with them; it was very costly in one sense. He extended his organization to bring in different people, knowing that we are a part of the bigger picture. So, the broader picture for me was being in the world and being part of the larger world too. That was part of the consciousness that started to be formed within me when I was eighteen. Probably where it really started to become more articulated for me was when I was in graduate school and started dealing with organizational theory at St. Mary's College in Winona, Minnesota. They had a unique program called Human Development; there were only three such programs in the United States around 1972. One was somewhere in California and another one was, I think, in Ohio. In fact, I was at the University of Minnesota telling them what I wanted to do in psychology around Maslow's work in the early seventies and they said, "What you want to do is great, Bill, but we don't do it here." Anyway, the professors and other people in this program at St. Mary's College were just phenomenal. I was exposed to a developing leading-edge consciousness by my professors. That's where the idea of transformation started to become more formulated for me. There was a wonderful book called *Social Philosophy*—it's out of print. The author's whole thing was about the connectedness of "we." He said there is no such thing as "I," in one sense; that basically, we are a "we" and we are inextricably intertwined with one another. I see all organizations as being part of a creative process.

I'm going to have to jump back. This point is going to be critical in order for me to make any other statements—if we're going to be talking about what it really means for me at a bottom level. My main thing is that each of us has as our essence a triune relationship. And that relationship is with ourselves, with others, and with whatever you want to call it—ultimate meaning, ultimate purpose, ultimate other. We all have an "essence-tial" essence as part of what we are—what it means to be human beings having an essential relationship with what I call the Divine Creative Process. And that means that we are all inextricably entwined in creation. That has significant ramifications for my philosophy/theology of work. Where I've generally given this presentation before is when I've done seminars called "The Theology of the Workplace." So for me it's imperative that we start transforming organizations to a consciousness that we are all really one—we are all tied to the Divine, and all that we do by way of work is really part of that creative process. We are in creation of each other—helping to build each other. No matter what we do—as you are doing your work right now and I am doing my practitioner work right now, you are helping me to reflect as you come to me. Theoretically, I'm helping you with an interview; in the process you are helping me as a focal point for me to further reflect and refine my thoughts and perspectives and perhaps even get this disseminated out somewhere. So that's where you and I are in an honest interaction and "commune-ication"—you help me, I help you. In business, I don't have any problem with the fact that people make money; we have to have money to sustain ourselves. I don't mean to oversimplify the world—it's terribly complex. But organizations for me are organizations of people, each of whom has this essential triune relationship. The more we become conscious of what I call our "essence-tial" triune relationship: my relationship with myself, my intricate inextricable relationship with you, and my inextricable relationship with the Divine Creative Process—the more elevated our work is in terms of consciousness and how we approach one another, the world, the products we bring to bear in the world and the products we don't bring to bear in the world. There are a lot of harmful products out there.

By the way, this concept of being inextricably intertwined is part and parcel of Christian theology and I make no bones about it—I came from a Catholic Christian tradition, and I spent a long time undercutting, or getting through the cultural overlays of Catholic Christianity. Most people experience Catholic Christianity almost exclusively in its cultural overlay, not in its theological underpinnings. I spent a long time getting to the spiritual underpinnings—and that is critical to my understanding. Again, if you're going to talk about being inextricably tied to the Divine, it goes way back for me. So, when does that start to have ramifications in terms of human community? I'm still on your question of where these things started to formulate. My Human Development degree is a cross between spiritual theology and developmental psychology, that's why I put that in there, it's a blending of the two.

I've always gone from practice to theory. I taught for two and a half years, then I took two years off. And then I taught for three more years and I took about three years off; I did some sideline work. And then I was a regional manager for a research firm for several years and then I took about eighteen months or a year and a half off. So, it's something that happens for me. What it is for me, I think, is staying in the "now moment"—I don't choose it; essentially, I end up selling everything I have to live. And I've done that more often than I care to. At the same time my value system is so engrained—that is, doing what I need to do when I need to do it, and I'll be taken care of—so it's a trusting and letting-go process.

Everything we do—everything—every interaction is always spiritual because I am connected with you in some way. Martin Buber, the great rabbi and philosopher, had a wonderful book called *I and Thou*. A classic statement was that every meeting is an encounter. Every time I connect with another person, even if it's just a glance on the street, at that moment I encounter *you*, which means this is a significant human interaction. It is significant in the sense that even if you and I don't stop and say hello or anything and just passed by, it is still in that moment an interaction. Obviously, the more communication that goes on—the greater the inter-action—the greater the encounter, if you will. But we are really all affected by everybody. That's part of it for me, that's something that I've been consciously developing various ways of thinking about—certainly becoming more sophisticated in terms of seeing the complexities and seeing how it plays out as each passing day goes by. And as far as becoming a practitioners in this, it becomes mind-boggling sometimes when I see the dynamics of what's going on and what is not going on—or what could be going on if people were only open to letting go of their barriers. We need barriers but we also need to let them go gradually as much as possible, and to see our connectedness.

I talk about this in organizations more indirectly. First of all, I don't have the financial backing right now to be able to say I think they can handle it for me to talk about it directly. I also think it's an imposition to talk about it too directly. But in organizations, I do talk about the managerial role as being a sacred trust. And I did that at Data General. I thought it would come back to haunt me—it never did—I was amazed. And when I first put it out there I said, "I'm going right out on a limb and I'm going to tell you what this stuff means to me." And I was talking to senior middle managers. Another approach I have with organizations is working with communications and how people relate to one another. So we talk about the authenticity of our communications. We talk about body language, we talk about double messages. The more I am consistent with who I am, just with myself, and then with you, I don't have to be overtly conscious of the spiritual dimension—the spiritual dimension is actually happening. Anytime we have authentic communication, or the more authentic our communication is, because they're inextricably intertwined, I don't have to have the consciousness of the Level Three. All I have to do is respond authentically to people; to the extent that I do that, our relationships are far more productive and creative work is going on. So my work, the practitioner part of me, is really helping people to be honest with themselves. A lot of what I do helps people to focus on who they really are; who they are in any given interaction, and what they want to say in that given interaction; it has to do with challenging people.

PROFILE: HARRISON OWEN

White male, age 53
President, H. H. Owen and Co.
M.A., Vanderbilt University

I guess there really was never a time that I wasn't interested in OT. My background is I am an Episcopal priest. I am basically a theologian, and what I was really interested in was on one level the function of the individual and culture in the ancient Near East. Sooner or later you've got to get beyond that kind of stuff and ask the question, "What's happening?" I was a pure academic at that point, and then we had a small thing called the Birmingham bombings, and civil rights, and I was in Tennessee at that point, and I found myself—it really wasn't a conscious act on my part—I found myself in the streets in the middle of all this. I came here to Washington and ran a large downtown community association. I was in West Africa for a while with the Peace Corps—Liberia—and worked with the local health care system, some local programs, and then the National Institute of Health and Veterans Administration and stuff like that. I don't know that I ever tried to say this before, but what I thought I was doing was going out to do something as opposed to making a buck. Around 1977, I was doing a seminar up at MIT—this is one of those things where they brought in a senior manager and they roasted you for six hours. Roasted—that's about the only way I can describe it. They gave you twenty minutes up front to say who you are and what you do. Whatever it was that you were doing was the subject of discussion. Anyhow, probably because the devil made me do it, I started by saying that really what I did was created myths and rituals. Actually, at that point I was running the senior-level executive development program for the VA. I was executive for their national advisory group, but what I was really doing was using all that as kind of a political operative—and it's a nice cover. If you're running an "academic program," you can go anywhere in Washington and do anything. So I was sometimes quite formally, but usually not, interfacing between the White House and other agencies and Congress and veteran's groups, whatever. Anyhow, that's why they had me there at MIT—I was to supposedly talk about that. I started out by saying what I did was create myths and ritual, and after defending that, I ended up just kind of talking on, as a likely story, about that for about six hours, using it more as a metaphor, but when I got through, what I discovered was that the metaphor was reality. It was one of those kind of blinding flashes of the obvious. What it did was integrate ten years of academic studies with ten more years of fussing around with systems, and out of that came a realization that for whatever reason, I seemed to be able to operate in what I guess you'd call a political environment in ways that my friends didn't understand. I would just put my fingers on one thing and push that button and all kinds of things would happen. My detractors had one way of talking about it, my friends said it was sort of magic. I really didn't understand what it was, but what I did understand was I could do it at very high levels of government.

Anyhow, bottom line was that by the end of that seminar I recognized, quite unconsciously, that I'd used everything I knew about myth, ritual and culture and kind of a basic understanding of what happens to large systems under the heading of transformation, although I wouldn't have called it that at that point. So, literally two or three weeks after I did that thing, I resigned my position at the VA, created my own company, and said that this is either black magic or there's something here, and I can't talk about it any more until I'm convinced there's really something here—something that I could state as a testable hypothesis, and apply it, and do it, and replicate it, and whatever. So then I did about two or three years of working with a string of clients where they typically hired me to spin up some crazy large-scale program or something. It was strategic planning, or it didn't make any difference what it was. And I took it as an occasion to look at their myths and rituals as a way of dealing with their cultures. So I did that for a while, and by the end of that—this would have been 1981—I was convinced that there really was something there, it was repeatable and it was a powerful way of looking at things.

What I found was that it's amazing how fast things changed. You can't hardly talk about an organization today without mentioning culture. In 1980, if you were to do that the execs would think you were trying to sell opera tickets or whatever. Terry Deal helped that one out a little bit. What I found was I could create a general theoretical structure that was predictive, which allowed me to operate with really large social systems. So, by 1981 or 1982 I was pretty well convinced that (1) there was a useful way to go here and (2) you could educate, you could help other people to do the same thing. I think there are certain basic things that are helpful. You have to trust your intuition, you have to be open to what people are saying, you have to be able to go beyond the structures and forms of things but in many ways it's a process of unlearning rather than learning.

Data goes only so far; the truth of the matter is that by the time you get all the data in and analyzed, the situation is so different than what you started with, it doesn't make any difference anyhow. So we literally need some very different ways, not only of working, but of conceptualizing what we're looking at. Anyhow, by 1981–82 I'd pretty well convinced myself that there was something here. I did a little writing in the area, submitted an article to *Organization Dynamics*, which was returned because everyone knew that organizational culture was too far out—nobody would believe this stuff. Anyhow, Terry Deal came out with his book and a lot of folks said, "Well, Terry's just written your book." All of a sudden it became legitimate to talk about culture. It was about that time that

Marilyn Ferguson had just finished *The Aquarian Conspiracy*, and things were sort of popping. Thought about transformation comes from anthropology and psychology and a variety of other things. It really hadn't been thought about, and certainly not applied, in an organizational setting before. I think for understandable reasons people were perhaps more enamored with the "Gee, isn't it wonderful?" side than "Let's take a full look at the thing." But, in any event, if culture was just barely acceptable, transformation was something that we know has got to be really weird. In talking to a friend of mine by the name of David Belisle, we were aware of a couple of things and number one was the theoretical box we were working in as consultants. With all due respect to Dick Beckhart and all the rest of the folks, change theory worked very well if you knew where you were and you knew where you wanted to get to, and then how to sequence it so that you could manage the change. But when you didn't know where you were and you had no idea where you were going to, and were just kind of hanging out, it's a very different situation, and there just weren't any boxes to put that in. So, what David and I did was to create one, "We don't have any idea what this is, but we'll just call this Organization Transformation." I don't know if I'm the one who coined that phrase. My story is that sitting on the lawn at Tarrytown, it would have been spring of 1981—I mean I know we had never thought of it before. People had talked about transformation before and people had talked about organizations. We said, "Well, hell, we have no idea what this is, we don't know what you do with it, but let's just capitalize it. It's a box, a sandbox, we don't know what it is. Maybe it's a practice, maybe it's a theory, we don't know."

For about nine months we did a weekly seminar, the two of us. Where we just kind of bent on this, until a whole mess of ideas really started to glue together about what seemed to us to be the process. At that juncture, right in the midst of all this, Martin Marietta, where David worked, was going crazy. In the system that I was working with, anything was fair game. So what we were really trying to do was to put together a likely story about what this was. In the spring of '82, the Boston regional ODN was having its springtime go, and Tom Chase put out a request for papers around the general subject of what do you do now that the "third wave" has hit; Toffler had just done that one. So David and I put in a paper which we called "Myth and Ritual as the Ground of Organizational Transformation." Totally unbeknownst to us, we ended up being the last paper at this thing and it was a three-day conference, and the first one was done by Linda Ackerman, Burns and Shannon. Their paper was entitled "Myth and Ritual and the Transformation of the New Army." Anyhow, what effectively happened was that the whole conference was bracketed by our two presentations. When it was all over, David and I hit the bar, and while we were sitting there, this queue of people started going by, saying, "What are you going to do with this"? My inclination was, basically nothing. I went back to Washington and kept getting calls. It was kind of a funny story, but at that juncture I said, "This is getting ridiculous." So I literally took thirty names at random out of the participant list of that conference and put together a letter which I got David and Linda and Frank Burns and Jim Shannon all to sign. What the letter said was that if the idea of Organization Transformation resonates anywhere in your head and you'd like to be party to figuring out what it means, let me hear from you. I figured that would be the end of it. Well, what happened was that over the course of the next four or five months I got something like 150 responses from as far away as Australia and a variety of other places. At that juncture I said, "I think I'm in deep tapicoa, no way am I going to answer all of these things, we obviously need a newsletter, I'm not sure what about, but we'll create a newsletter." A kind of side piece on the local mythology is that I sent that letter out on some letterhead, which just said TWG. What it really meant was The Washington Group, and it was a consulting firm that David Belisle and I had created—we'd never done anything with it. The corporation eventually lapsed, and all that was left was the letterhead. TWG literally meant nothing, just three letters on a letterhead. So anyhow one thing led to another and somewhere in there Tom Chase said we ought to have a conference and that sounded like a reasonable idea, so I sent out another newsletter that said, "Well, we're going to hold the first national symposium on Organization Transformation at a time and place we've got to figure out." Lo and behold, a year later at Durham, New Hampshire, 250 folks literally from all over the world showed up, and it's kind of run from there.

The phrase Organization Transformation was clearly in the air and it very clearly provided a theoretical frame of reference, and I guess honestly a very practical frame of reference. Those were very exciting and very anxious days, because what you find yourself doing is just constantly going to the edges of whatever it was that passed for legitimate organizational theory, and knowing that that wasn't working, or if it was working, it was only working in fairly prescribed areas, and you just had to get beyond that.

Where has it all led me? Well, I guess somewhere along the line I asked myself the question, "What gets transformed?"—the word would tell you that it's not formed—it's something that goes from one form to another. And so, having "culture" and then "transformation," the next thing for me was literally "spirit." From that day until this day I don't have any idea what spirit is. I experience organizations as spirit communities. But then there's also a conceptual side which is that if you happen to be the CEO of a 70,000-employee multinational thing operating in 50 countries, and try to think about that in any way that rational management science would allow you to think about it, you're going to go crazy. First of all the sheer numbers of people, then the countries, then the cultural differences, then everything else that is happening in the world. It seemed to me that what we really needed to do was to have some conceptual ways to handle large, complex, fast-moving systems. It's also true with very small systems like the family, because I think the dynamics are the same. Well, I was really working with large systems, and I think my work has brought me at this point (A) to take spirit quite seriously and (B) to hopefully start to say something intelligent about how spirit in fact works in large systems.

I wrote two essays, one in *Transforming Work* and one in *Transforming Leadership*, both books edited by John Adams. I guess in those two, particularly the second one, I sort of came out of the closet on the question of spirit; and then with *Spirit*, the book itself.

It seems that every year we've had one of these symposiums on Organizational Transformation. Starting about five years ago, I came to the conclusion that never again would I do your formal standard meeting. My experience was that you go to these damn things and anything that was really worthwhile always happened during the coffee breaks. Anything that was substantive in nature, by and large, had been written down before, or could have been written down before, so why not read it? And furthermore, since the agenda and papers had been established six-to-nine months before, the likelihood was that it was basically irrelevant to whatever was going on today anyhow. Not totally but pretty close to it. I joked with friends, "The only thing that's useful at conferences is the coffee break, so let's just have coffee breaks." So what started just as an experiment, ended up being a very powerful and repeatable format. The only thing that everybody knows when they come is when it starts, when it ends, who's coming, and what they're interested in. Then, using a real high-tech thing which is known as the "camp sign-up board," everybody is invited to spend a second with themselves and identify what's their point of passion, what's their interest at the moment, give it a short title and put it on a placard. Then they can stand up and they've got two minutes in front of a microphone to say, "I'm interested in—" Put it up on the wall.

This just goes on until nobody has anything else to say. And then what we do is say OK, stand up and walk around and take a look at any of those that you like, and write your name on them. Then whoever put it up there in the first place is responsible for negotiating a time and place. We start out with this long sheet of butcher paper, like forty feet long, and just mark it into the days, and just put those placards wherever they would fall, and that's our schedule. Well, the first time we did this, it took a group of about 85 two and a half hours to create a 5-day agenda. The next time we did it, it took a group of 150 an hour and a half. The next time we did it we had a group of about 95, and we did it in an hour and ten minutes. Last year we had a group of about 90 and we did it in an hour flat. These are not basically the same folks, except for maybe ten of them. I think part of its success is that the mechanisms we're appealing to are so basic that people don't have to learn about them—it's so simple. And then you say, "What do you do with conflict?" What you ordinarily do with conflicts, you negotiate them. But instead of taking a whole group's time to get that done, if you and I want to get together around a particular issue and there's four others who are interested in that issue but also want to go to some other meeting, what we do is those involved have a fast huddle and we decide what we're going to do.

Ordinarily, with a group of 100 or more, we would have maybe 25 different substantive areas of discussion. It can run all the way from the addictive organization to taking a major organization as a case study to death and dying. But because everybody is there from a point of passion, the thing starts really going critical very fast, and if it doesn't, since everybody created it, nobody has any problem with saying "forget it." Or, what happens equally often is that you get into a group and although the title said "blank," it's quite clear that there are at least two issues, and maybe three. Don't sit around and fight over it, create three new groups— no problem. You are now responsible for time and space—create it, use it, and make it work for you. People who have been through this thing say things like, "You know, I've never learned as much or as quickly." It doesn't make any sense at the level of what we would call rational plotting out of the bodies, but at the level of spirit it makes perfect sense. People find exactly what they need when they need it.

It's not just the OT crowd I've done this with. I've done it with very straight, pin-stripe, strategic types. Exactly the same format. I don't include some of the hugs and squeezes and whatever, but that's just how you format it in the culture. You kinda hafta sweet talk 'em into it. We've gotten more and more efficient every year in terms of the OT things. I coined what turned out to be the four immutable principles that works for meetings. They are: whoever comes are the right people, whatever happens is the only thing that could have, whenever it starts is the right time, and when it's over it's over. That doesn't mean you don't prepare, that doesn't mean you don't make the best effort to get certain people there, but when you start, those principles will apply.

So one of the things that's happened is I know I can walk into any group and if they're clear on the area they want to get into, we can get them up and running at high levels of performance. We've used this for product development. I won't mention the corporation, but they wanted to produce an interactive computer-based order entry system for their customers, and the MIS people said, "Yeah, you can't do that—it's gonna cost you a million dollars and a year and a half." We took a volunteer group of twenty-three people—we said that in order to do something like that, we need marketing sales, MIS (Management Information Systems), customer relations, whatever. We just sent out an invitation across the corporation that said, "Hey, this is what we're going to do: we're going to create this software—and these are the kinds of people we think we need to play in this game. Now if you meet any of those requirements and would like to play, come." Nobody was ordered to come. "And furthermore, if you don't fit in any of those categories, come too but be prepared to say what it is you think you can contribute. Nobody is going to be ordered to do this—A; and B—everybody is responsible for their regular job, OK?" Well, this group, doing basically what we were doing at the OT symposium, created a working system in eight days flat. They took it through the beta test, had a product for delivery in three months, and for a total out-of-pocket expense of $35,000.

It's interesting, when we got through with that, the company had a problem—everybody wanted to do it because of what these folks reported. I interviewed them all afterwards and they reported that they had never had so much fun, worked so hard, felt so challenged, and felt so fulfilled. You can't operate at that high level forever, but there are situations when you can, and should, and then maybe you ought to rest—so you learn how to pace. Anyhow, that ends up being, I think, a very practical sort of thing. So, to try to understand that so that you can "rationally manage" it—you really can't do it. Although you can describe, after the fact maybe, in journals—we've done a lot of that—about what happened minute-by-minute, second-by-second, the interrelationships and everything else, there is no reason to believe that any of that will replicate in detail. It will replicate as a pattern, so it has to be thought of as a pattern and, what's really patterning, I think, is of spirit.

Spirit is what transforms. I mean, I would start out with the bold statement that what is, is spirit, which comes to form in time and space—spirit is what it is. If you ask me what spirit is, I don't have any idea. "Open space" is the natural process through which spirit flows, and by recognizing that natural process you can help it.

One of the things you know is going into open space scares the shit out of you. I don't care who you are. And just parenthetically, anybody who says that they "transform" organizations without pain—hasn't been there. I mean, this is my opinion, they don't know what they're talking about, because what you're really talking about, whether it's that community that just had the superhighway put through the neighborhood, or the corporation that just had its financing cut off, or whatever it is—they're through. So there are a lot of things that one can do—not in a step-one-two-three kind of way, but there are a lot of things that you can learn to do, and help people to do for themselves and for each other.

PROFILE: BRYANT ROLLINS

Black male, age 51
Chairman/Chief Executive Officer
Mountaintop Ventures, Inc.
B.A., Northeastern University
Journalism Fellowship, University of Massachusetts
Currently writing a book on Operation Push with Jesse Jackson

The first work I ever did in the field of Human Resources and Organization Development was as a practitioner. I got involved during the Civil Rights movement—in Roxbury. I was a reporter for the Boston Globe. And the Globe had a policy, at that time, which was limited to one person, myself. I was the only Black reporter, and the policy statement was that Black reporters couldn't cover what was happening in Roxbury because they couldn't be objective. I went crazy around that and said, "You'll lose your only Black reporter in six months unless your policy changes." They wouldn't change it. I mean it was absolutely irrational—purely racist. So they had white folks covering those events because they could be objective. So, I founded a paper in Roxbury for a couple of years, and then went to work for the Urban League. What we did at the Urban League, which was essentially the beginning of a twenty-year journey for me, was try to figure out what kind of role we could play in the city to help support the transformation of local organizations. We got away from the traditional Urban League role, which was to find jobs for middle-class folks. We became what we called "The New Urban League," and we hoisted a black and green flag over the building. Whitney Young came in and threatened to throw us out of the Urban League. But we decided that we were going to be gadflies in the community; go in and work with existing organizations to try to help them to become more effective. There was a lot of money coming into Black communities then, "War on Poverty" money— city money—being wasted. There were a lot of unresolved conflicts in the community.

So I got involved with some Organization Development people at Boston College. I didn't even know that that was a field at that time until somebody said, "These guys know how to look at an organization and tell you how to fix it." And I began to work with them in 1968, and I had some personal growth experiences. We began to develop some clients in Roxbury, organizations that were struggling. And we began to change them— we began to work with their conflict-management skills, their planning skills, their decision-making skills, and I saw the successes of these folks who were OD people, organization psychologists. I became aware that change was possible for me, and I didn't need to think of myself as being stuck. I became aware that I could take charge of myself, or I could get help from others who would support me in going in the direction that I wanted to go. And I became aware that I could make decisions. Now I grew up in Roxbury, my father was a plumber and my mother a seamstress. My father was not a union plumber because Black people were not allowed in the union at that time. He worked for the government, and they paid a different scale. So we were poor—you know, you get on a track, and if you're lucky you get on a good one—but not much hope for change, personal change. Well, the fact that I worked for the Globe was completely coincidental. It was an accident, and I never expected it. So, I never took any personal pleasure in being a Black professional. It didn't feel like I'd done anything. It's like I skidded on some grease and went in that direction and I was lucky. It wasn't until I got involved in these kinds of processes that I began to understand that I could play a role and needed to play a role in my own future; that I could make decisions, that I could grow consciously, that I could set the direction and have a vision for where I wanted to go, create the environment where I could get there, and find supports. I found that I could do whatever I had to do, and that it could be a conscious process. I discovered that there were things that got in the way of my achieving my vision that I could manage. All of this suddenly unfolded for me when I was in my twenties. I learned a lot of things—about the need for a vision, about the effect of conscious versus subconscious processes—a whole range of things that I had never thought about before. And it was happening not just for me, but we were out working in the community, and I saw it happening with organizations. I saw organizations like War on Poverty that one month would be stuck—fighting, rangling, pulling guns on each other. Even with million-dollar grants, the people would come into an anti-poverty meeting off the streets, not be able to manage their conflicts, and about to go to war with each other in the meeting. I saw things like that change in six months to a point where all year they could manage their conflicts and were dealing with each other in a humane fashion. I participated in the processes that helped that to happen. It was happening to me and I saw it happening in the community. I saw new institutions put into place in the community.

So, I've experienced transformation and I've seen it happening. It led me first to keep being a consultant to help these things continue to happen. So, for the last twenty years I've done some consulting, even when I've had full-time jobs. I worked at the *New York Times*, I taught in a journalism program at Columbia, I ran the *Amsterdam News*—these were all full-time jobs. While I was doing this work, four or five times a year I would take off and do some consulting somewhere as part of my contract with these organizations. I just never stopped because it was so gratifying. And I've worked on my own development, through psychoanalysis, through all kinds of processes for myself—so I continued the work.

In 1979, I was editor of the *Amsterdam News*, and I had a fight with the publisher. It was a political disagreement over Koch and whether or not to support the Koch administration. The publisher was a Koch supporter and we had an ongoing six-month battle, and finally he fired me. I decided then that I'd never work for anybody again and that I wanted to dedicate myself to changing things. I set up Mountaintop Ventures. I worked by myself for five or six years, with the help of people who I associated with over the years—a lot of them NTL people. I was just lucky to come into contact with those folks at that time—they had the right thing for me. A lot of my practice and theory around change comes from NTL people. I've worked with some of the really good people at NTL over the years.

Where did I get the name, Mountaintop Ventures? It came from Martin Luther King, Jr.'s address where he says, "I've been to the mountaintop." So, Mountaintop Ventures is a metaphor for a process more than anything else. What Mountaintop is, primarily, is a series of relationships. That begins with a core group on the inside. The people who work full-time or on a fairly regular basis with Mountaintop have a commitment to work on race and gender issues within themselves and among ourselves as a group of people, and then by extension out into the world. In doing that, what we've committed to is working on those issues in relationship to other people and in relationship to institutions. Our mission statement says that we are about making a historic difference. So by extension, we're working with changing the world to some degree.

We think the transformation begins like Martin said, "All real change begins on the inside." We believe that the commitment that we've made with each other is a commitment to work on our own racism and sexism in all kinds of ways, thus diminishing the effects of those things on our own relationships, and on our work—and then to work those issues out in the world. And then, by extension, other "isms." What that implies is transforming ourselves almost on a daily basis.

The Mountaintop process is, in fact, a series of events, practices, concepts, experiences, and strategies that transform organizations by intervening in those systems through processes that focus on race and gender. That's the point of entry conceptually. It's interesting, because it's also personal. I have found a way to grow as a human being. That same experience that I've had over the years in looking at my own racism and its effect on me—devaluing myself, and my own sexism and its effect on me—devaluing women; to the extent that I've learned more about and experienced more of myself in those areas, I've become a much richer human being—a better person. I think the same way about systems. Whenever I have something that I can't figure out about myself, the first place I look is, "Am I thinking or behaving in a way that's racist or sexist?" Now there are a lot of other ways I could think about those things, but that's where I go first, because they're deeply engrained, they are very powerful for me—they are sure—I know that if I go look there, I'll find out what the problem is; it works every time. As we work with systems, we find the same thing. To the extent that systems are aware and skilled at managing and relating to people of color and women, is the degree to which they are becoming more humane, more effective systems, more flexible.

PROFILE: MICHAEL SHANDLER

White male, age 42

Founder and Head of Vision Action Associates

Ed.D., Leadership and Organization Development
University of Massachusetts

I came to be interested in OT by being frustrated in a lot of organizations that I've been a part of, basically. It was like the Dark Ages—really, people didn't know what to do. It's not that they were "bad" people, it's just that the systems that they were stuck in basically gave rise to mediocrity and trapped them. Very often they didn't know how to get out of it and became victims of these systems. I was frustrated by that. Almost all of the organizations that I was a part of, including such places as the university, fall into that. I had an experience when I was the director of a seventy-five-person organization and I began doing team-building. I didn't know what I was doing and it didn't work. But I could see well enough that if I knew what I was doing, something could really change. So, it was after that that I got into OD as opposed to OT, and for me the two sort of blend into one almost—but OD being more the Old School.

Before I continue, I want to say one thing. A lot of what's going on in OT is really sort of fuzzy and there is a reaction out there in real organizations to the fuzziness of it. I think that OT has to be very careful about that because it can be seen as so much on the cutting edge that it no longer communicates that it's basically all of these great ideas of individuals. The area that I'm interested in and in fact, specialize in is looking for those places in organizations where you're asking certain kinds of basic questions. Let me give you some examples that might be more helpful. Three weeks ago, I worked with the chairman of the board—and his direct staff—of a Fortune 500 company called AM International in Chicago. This came as a result of a request from 140 of the managers worldwide. They requested that the chairman of the board and his direct staff come up with a vision that would include: what are the basic values of the culture of AM International? This also would include: what kind of business are we in? So, we got together and we spent three days with this top management group in which we articulated a vision statment. The vision statement came out of the considerations and work of all of these twelve individuals. I had given them a preparation book in which they each had actually articulated their own vision statements. We then put all twelve of those together—we had twelve of them up on the wall. From there we condensed it down over a period of several hours into one statement, which they adopted as the corporate vision. Then I said to them, "Look, this is a very neat statement—it's actually a great turn-on, but my fear about it is that this statement can just gather dust. We all got high doing this exercise and it was just great, and when we leave here, the thing that can happen is just business as usual. The main thing that we now have to do is to articulate how do we operationalize this vision—in other words, how do we take this vision from being a 'pie-in-the-sky' statement to something that we can measure, that we can create results against to measure progress within certain time parameters?" So, we came up with a set of goals. We came up with eight different goals in different areas of the vision that included both the business side and the culture side. Once we had done that, we said, "OK, that's the vision and those are the goals that will operationalize this vision; now which members of this team will champion each of these goals? So, we chose goal champions—visionary goal champions. We also chose the roles that the other team members were going to play in relations to these goal champions. So every goal had a goal champion, and everybody else on the team was given, and also assumed a particular responsibility as a support person or as an expert helper. Then we took a look at what are called "critical success factors." "That's our vision and these are our goals, what are the critical success factors that have to show up in each goal area?" So critical success factors are those things that must be done, and must be done well in order to succeed in a particular goal—in creating particular results. When we had done that, we then took a look at the dynamics of the team, and asked them very basic questions like, "What is the stuff that gets in the way of us in this room truly functioning as an inspired team to pull off that vision?" And all kinds of answers showed up. There were all sort of personal difficulties with people, there were structural problems within the organization, there were certain fears that people had about being punished if they told the truth, etc. And so we came up with a set of ground rules about how this team agreed to behave with each other, how they would hold each other's feet to the fire around certain behaviors. So for me that's an example of OT in practice, that kind of intervention. Once the chairman of the board and his team had gone through this process, it became very obvious that the next step for them would be to enroll the next level of management, which is about 140 other managers. We're going back to Chicago, and ten of us are going to do a process involving all 150 of these managers to get them exposed to the vision, the goals, and ground rules, and to enroll them in it—to help them to feel like they are a part of it. They'll nominate themselves to action teams to actually help in the attainment of their goals. Last year I did forty of these interventions with different companies all over the country.

My intervention includes the notion of 100-percent responsibility. I'm going to share with you what that is very briefly. The notion of 100-percent responsibility goes something like this, and I want you to understand that this is not the "truth," it's a working premise. It's straight from science and means that you assume that the universe works in a certain way, you act as though it does, and you get a certain result, even if it's actually not true. So, 100-percent responsibility is the following: "I'm 100-percent responsible for the results that show up, whether I actually am responsible or not—I act as though I'm 100-percent responsible for the success of this entire team, or this entire organization." The truth is that you and I know that organizations are very complex and that one person can't do it alone. But the notion is that I'm 100-percent responsible and the paradox is that I can't do it alone. It's an operating premise that a person walks around with in their minds. Now, Organization Transformation occurs when a critical mass of individuals in an organization really walks around saying, "I'm 100-percent responsible and circumstances and other individuals have zero percent responsibility" even though that's not the truth. They walk around and they act as though it is true—and then they act out of that. I think it is very much an Organization Transformation contribution.

I believe that we are all interconnected and this doesn't contradict that. I mean I absolutely accept our interconnection, without any question. That's why I talk about the expression in OT of the whole human systems philosophy, which very much accepts that we are all interconnected. That all systems, even from a basic earth level, all the way out, including human beings, are interconnected. It's the paradox of adopting an attitude of acting as though you were responsible even though you know it's not the truth. I accept that I'm interconnected, I act as though I were 100-percent responsible for all of the results that show up in my life. I act out of that responsibility because it gives me a choice about the actions that I can take to basically foster good for the whole. Whereas, if I say, "Well, I'm just at the behest of circumstances here—there's nothing I can do," I've basically disempowered myself. So, it is a paradox of accepting the unity, and at the same time acting as though you're responsible, even though you know it's not true. This might sound like an ego trip, but I'm one of the founding thinkers in the area of visionary planning. I don't label myself as an OT practitioner, and I generally do not like labels, because labels tend to confine people. There are many aspects of OT that I do not wish to be associated with, which is not to say that I'm not sympathetic. I'm very sympathetic to the endeavors of the field, but in some ways I do not want to be associated with it. I do not want my clients to think of me as an OT practitioner. I want them to see me as somebody who is truly helpful to them and their endeavors rather than having my own agendas. And OT could be seen as having too much of it's own agenda. So, I'm very client-centered in that sense.

Last year I spent approximately 150 days doing presentations and workshops, and they were primarily in-house. When I say in-house, I mean that they're usually inside organizations with management teams. The titles of those presentations differ. The primary one that I do is called "Planning for Inspired Performance," which deals with whole co-creation of the vision, setting goals, the ground rules. A secondary piece, which is sometimes included in that program, is around the whole notion of leadership—visionary leadership. A third theme is the notion, that I've also talked about, called 100-percent responsibilty. Another theme is guaranteeing value in advance. I could share with you a short story. An old man of about eighty-five was on his deathbed. His whole family was around, everybody knew that he was going to die. He called his wife to his side and with his last remaining strength he pulled himself up and whispered a bunch of things to her and then he laid down and shortly after that he passed away. Well, his sons and daughters were very keen to know what his last words were to his wife—to their mother. She said, "He wanted you kids to not make the same mistake that he made." And they said, "Well, what's that, Mom?" and she said, "Well, he'd been reflecting on the value of his life when he was too old to do anything about it." In other words, there were certain results that had shown up in his life, but he was too old to go back and change some of the stuff that he had regrets about. So, she said, "He wanted you kids to know that the right time to take stock of your life," and this is a metaphor for managers, "is when you are beginning." Not when it's too late, not when you can't do anything about the past. So, when you start, realize what your purpose is—realize what the results and the values are that you're trying to create, and then go about doing it. It is kind of a vision, but it's about putting your word on the line and guaranteeing the value that you're going to create even before you start—it's about living your life from that point of view. You start by saying, "I'm going to create inspired performance, my life is about inspired performance, I'm not going to wait and see if inspired performance shows up, I'm actually going to create it—and I'm saying right now that I'm going to create it." So, it's putting your word on the line, and going forward with it.

PROFILE: JOHN SIMMONS

White male, age 50

President, Participation Associates

Adjunct Professor, Labor Management Relations
University of Massachusetts
Executive Editor, *Workplace Democracy*
Ph.D., Economics, Oxford University

I felt there had to be a better way to manage people than I'd experienced as an employee and as a manager. While on projects in the Third World, I also saw that the major drawback to effective and efficient use of resources in those countries was management. The World Bank where I worked provided all kinds of great technical assistance and funds, but the management of the projects and the management of the ministries we worked through was very inadequate. So I could see the real drawbacks from the management standpoint. The insights that led me to my work have to do essentially with empowering people to take more control over their work. People are being mismanaged and they know it. They need to be empowered to speak up and take more control and change themselves in the process.

For me it's pretty simple. In Organizational Transformation, as I have defined it, senior management has to buy into a set of core values that encourage the empowerment of all the people in the organization, including unions if they exist.

My philosophy is based on the importance of core values in improving organizational performance. Those core values are honesty, participation, trust, cooperation, fairness, and respect for individual differences. When those values are successfully implanted in an organization's culture, the organization has higher performance, better working conditions, and greater opportunity for sustained growth. One other reason why it's important is that it is a process that empowers people to take more control of their lives. It's sort of a "bill of rights" in the workplace. Most people have to give up those "rights" when they go through the factory gates.

PROFILE: SHIRLEY STETSON-KESSLER

White female, age 40
Vice President, Mountaintop Ventures, Inc.
M.Ed., Human Resources Development and Management Training

Where the theorist part of me comes into play in terms of what I do is my belief that organizations cannot and will not transform unless individuals do. If an organization takes it upon itself to decide to transform and individuals do not, there will be a parting of the ways of one sort or another. My growth and develoment internally has been a process of personal transformation. Through this I have been able to comprehend what it is that I want to do and be in the world. So, the whole idea of transformation was first put to me as a youngster—that my job was to grow up and be something. When I discovered that there is no destination, I began to realize that I feel much more comfortable with the notion of transformation because it means I can keep turning myself inside out forever and never be finished. If I have to "develop," it sounds like there's closure. That at some point I'll be "cooked"; like I did it and now I'm done, now I don't have to do anything else. On the other hand, I don't believe that I can be fully "transformed"; I am unlimited. I believe that organizations are the same way. I believe that there is a way to think so that change does not become something that we're afraid of; it becomes something that we'd like to move toward and be a a part of. In the course of the work that I do, I talk incessantly about these ideas.

I consider myself to be an Organization Transformation practitioner and I'm concerned with having the technology match the capacity of the human factor—that is, having the head and the pocketbook of the organization connected to the heart of the organization. So, transformation to me is something that's all-encompassing and takes into consideration all aspects of whatever the system might be. I used to be an Organization Development professional and my focus was much more on time-and-motion studies and organizing the flow of an office—very much more piece-oriented.

From my own growth experience, I view the world as a mirror of my own life—which is very spiritual. My view is also a pragmatic reflection of my training in psychology. It's become an exercise in understanding who I am in the world. A lot of what I have experienced as a person is that it's very, very hard to be affirmed in this place and time in history. And it's my goal to be affirmed. I understand that I have to feel that way on the inside and then I have to accept that experience on the outside. Every time I encounter a situation where I, for some reason, can't accept that I'm OK, I realize that there's transformation work to be done. I see that happening with other people and in organizations. I see it so many times a day that it's demoralizing; I can't sleep until I do something about it. So I'm driven from the inside-out and from the outside-in. I guess my family experience is very much responsible. I had a very affirming childhood. When I went outside the cloister of my home, I realized that something wasn't the same. When I began to feel taken advantage of, and hurt, then I made it my business to find out why. "What's the matter—what's going on out here?" When I see other women and people of color, or anybody who's different for any reason, being treated as though they're not OK, I realize that what's happening to that person is also happening to me. My view of the world is that I am only a cell in the body of humanity.

I am a highly intuitive person. I don't know where that came from, I just hit the planet that way. What I trust most is my intuition and I don't often say that because it gets me into trouble. I was a straight-"A" student all through school. Teachers would ask me how I knew the answers to math problems, etc., and it would be excruciating because I just knew the answer and I didn't necessarily know the process, or how I got the answer; of course, they thought I cheated. So I came to understand that there was this thing called intuition. And I didn't really care what anybody called it, I knew that I had something that worked when I just relaxed and let my inner voice speak. The whole idea of transformation just makes sense to me from personal experience.

Basically, what our consulting firm, Mountaintop Ventures, is all about is to make historical change through people. We know that every time there's one person who feels better about himself or herself, it's taking care of another piece of the whole, so it's important to us. The one person that we might spend a lot of time with could be someone who'd influence hundreds of people. Sometimes it's a judgment call whether to spend time with a person in an orgnaization. Usually when I need to make such a decision, I feel sad, because I may make a decision that I will regret; but I'm human too and I accept that part.

SUMMARY

Transformation as seen through the eyes of these fourteen people is indeed fascinating. All of the participants seem to be doing work that would make the workplace not merely tolerable for an organization's members, but a place of excitement in which an individual has a bit of creative license—a community in which an individual can feel supported, important and whole.

It was interesting to see how each individual differed in her/his emphasis and concerns, and how each one interpreted and used OT. The idea that spirituality can figure to make an organization better seemed important for several of the participants. Many of them came from some sort of spiritual or highly conscious background which led them into an interest in Organization Transformation.

John Adams took post-doctoral courses in physiology and endocrinology to add to his knowledge-base concerning how individuals create stress for themselves. This led to his deeper understanding of the processes involved in change. Norma Jean Anderson is involved in the ministry her husband started. She speaks of the concept of "renewing minds" and she mentions the personal spiritual path that she and members of her family have chosen. Then there is Jean Bartunek, who tells the story of the changes and turmoil in the Catholic church. She discusses how dealing with these changes brought her to a heightened awareness in Organization Transformation. Donald Carew's heightened awareness alerted him to how society was espousing one set of values and acting in ways that opposed those values; he calls it a dichotomy and identifies it as a big part of the problems that organizations experience. His work is, as he calls it, an attempt to "democratize" the workplace. Katharine Esty's interest in OT stemmed from her work in the psychological field. She is interested in how individuals transform and how, when that process goes awry for someone, an interested party can step in and help. This has led to her work with health organizations and, finally, into organizations as a consultant with a "systems" perspective. Allen Gordon refers to his work with the North Carolina Institute of Behavior as an attempt to bring the use of spirituality into organizations. All of the people interviewed have backgrounds that seem to lead them naturally into the field of OT.

It is interesting to note that all of the participants were adults or near adults during the turmoil of the 1960s. They all had a first hand look at a variety of new ways of thinking. Perhaps this made it easier to apply a heightened awareness of the dynamics of turmoil to the chaos faced by organizations today. Norma Jean Anderson alludes to this, as does Harrison Owen. Jean Bartunek mentions it in connection with the Catholic church, Don Carew mentions his experiences with segregation in college, and Bryant Rollins discusses his involvement in the civil rights movement in Roxbury.

There is a wide sprectum to the ways in which individuals in this study apply OT in their work. Some lean towards defining and applying spiritual concepts while others simply keep abreast of the ongoing conversations/debates and stick to OD kinds of interventions becasue they are viewed as being perhaps more credible.

There are some obvious differences in how these individuals go about doing OT work and how their various projects tie into their views of Organizational Transformation. This is, indeed, a richly mixed "bag" of people! There are, however, some common themes and strains of meaning and theory among them. The following chapters will explore those commonalities as well as some of the obvious differences.

3

Themes

An important technique for making sense of qualitative data is to examine the themes that emerge. The primary purpose of this chapter is to take a look at those themes. The chapter examines how participants in the study identify themselves (theorists vs. practitioners) and takes a look at participant philosophies, definitions, attitudes about OT, and meanings.

Meanings have to do with participant understanding—how they make sense of the phenomenon. Participants were asked the following questions:

- What is the difference between "theorists" and "practitioners"? What are you—a theorist or a practitioner?
- What does Organization Transformation mean to you (i.e., your definition for OT?)
- What adjectives, nouns, metaphors, or other descriptors would you use to describe an organization that has been transformed?
- Why is there such a thing as OT?
- What is the single most distinguishing aspect, objective, or purpose of OT?
- How would you summarize your philosophy about organizations? Can you relate that to any particular school of thought or philosophy?

A number of themes emerged from the participant's responses to these questions. First, let us examine how participants identify themselves: as theorists and/or practitioners of Organization Transformation.

OT THEORISTS/PRACTITIONERS

The first questions—"What is the difference between theorists and practitioners?" and "What are you, a theorist or a practitioner?"—elicit amazingly similar responses. Most participants make a distinction between the two; however, at the same time they express a belief that OT practitioners must also be theorists and, conversely, that theorists must have some practical experience.

Adams says that theorists are the people who are developing concepts, ideas, value systems, etc. That the development of values clarification is also a part of theory development. Practitioners are the people who are using some of those ideas in their work. Often they are the same people. Adams states that he is both theorist and practitioner—and in about equal measure.

Carew believes that most people interested in Organization Transformation are both theorists and practitioners. Major writers in the field, people who are putting together definitions, ideology and concepts about OT, lean more towards theory—even though they might also be practitioners. A practitioner, according to Carew, is someone who focuses more on doing as opposed to thinking about Organization Transformation. Carew acknowledges that he is perhaps more a practitioner than a theorist.

Gordon states that a theorist is a person who spends a lot of time researching, putting out hypotheses, and coming up with ideas as to how something can be accomplished. The practitioner, on the other hand, is the one who implements, who actually goes out and makes the thing happen. Gordon identifies himself as a practitioner.

Johnston says that he is both a theorist and a practitioner of Organization Transformation. He is what he calls "a practical theorist." According to Johnston, a practitioner is somebody who consciously or unconsciously applies theories and concepts of Self and Organization Transformation and Development in making interventions in organizations. Whether conscious of it or not, every practitioner operates on some theory; therefore, he or she is both a theorist and a practitioner—they are inseparable.

Stetson-Kessler also classifies herself as both practitioner and theorist. However she says that she is more a practitioner than a theorist. Stetson-Kessler believes that a theorist is someone who thinks and talks about what

Organization Transformation might be and does a lot of conceptual work and analyses, whereas a practitioner is somebody who is out there living, doing and experiencing the way organizations transform.

Table 3.1
What Are You—A Theorist or a Practitioner?

Both, But More a Practitioner	Both, But More a Theorist	Equally a Practitioner and a Theorist	Either a Practitioner (P) or a Theorist (T)
		X	
X			
	X		
X			
			P
X			
		X	
		X	
		X	
X			
X			
X			
			P
X			

All fourteen participants' responses are summarized in Table 3.1. As the table shows, all but two of the participants indicate that they are some blend of theorist and practitioner.

PERSONAL PHILOSOPHIES

Given the kinds of personal insights provided by those who were interviewed, a discussion of their personal philosophies seems the logical next step. During most of the interviews, both questions in the "Personal Philosophy" section of the Interview Guide were asked together as one question. Again, the questions are:

• How would you summarize your philosophy about organizations?
• Can you relate that to any particular school of thought or philosophy?

All but one of the participants respond to at least one of the two questions. Some participants focus their entire response on only one of the questions and others answer both.

Robert Johnston contends that we are all members of one mind, and that there are fundamentally two major forces within that one mind: yin and yang. One is masculine and one is feminine. According to Johnston, not only are we of one mind, we are also all connected. In addition, we are all eternal; we just don't remember that we are eternal. When we were conceived and went through the throes of all of the involuntary conditioning that started very shortly after our conception in our mothers' wombs, we forgot what we are—unless, of course, we were lucky and born into a family that somehow had carried on that remembrance of who and what we are in the Omniverse. Johnston says that his philosophy is related to that of the Kabbalists, the Jewish mystics. On the Far Eastern side, he borrows from the philosophy of the Taoists and Tantrists. He also incorporates Sheldrake's biology, Sir Jon Smut's holism, the transpersonal psychologies of people like Carl Jung, Roberto Assagioli, Ken Wilbur, and Stanislav Grof into his personal philosophy. Theories of quantum physicists such as David Bohm and the cognitive psychologies of Julian and Richard Davidson are also part of Johnston's philosophy. Johnston states that he has integrated Eastern and Western philosophies and psychologies in a unique way.

William Kueppers, like Johnston, talks about human interconnection, which is part of what he terms an "inextricable triune relationship." He believes that all humans are inherently in service to one another whether or not they are aware of it.

Harrison Owen believes that his personal philosophy is also eclectic, deriving from the fields of anthropology, psychology, theology, comparative religion, organization theory, theoretical physics, new biology, neurophysiology, classical Hebrew, and ancient mythology. He says, "I tell stories, and any good storyteller basically uses material so that there's a point of connection." Owen summarizes his philosophy about organizations as follows:

An organization is two or more gathered together to do something. At spirit level, an organization is an aggregate—a field of spirit. An optimally functioning organization is one that gets the job done with a certain amount of joy and celebration.

Bryant Rollins discusses his philosophy as being spiritual, religious, political, and impacted by his parents and environment as he grew up.

It's everything from a sense of universal values to some qualities and characteristics that my mother and father taught me, and it's everything in-between. It's democracy, and capitalism, and Judeo-Christian beliefs. It's holistic and it's also compartmentalized. It's psychological, I think it's spiritual, it's religious and it's political. We were poor, and I'm sure that had an effect on my belief systems; so it's economic to that degree. For me, however, the most powerful influence is specifically race and gender, with all of these other things interplaying; that is, my own personal life experiences were most powerfully affected by those two things. The fact that I was a Christian is less important to me, and the fact that I am an American is less important to me; the fact that I was born a boy-child and the fact that I was born a Black person are dramatically more significant to me than any of those other things; they had tremendous impact on my philosophy.

Michael Shandler talks about the impact of OD, family systems therapy and intuition on his thinking about organizations. He states that OD is definitely a strong influence, particularly the strategic planning aspects and T-group work. However, more on the cutting edge is the notion of human systems thinking. Shandler was trained as a family therapist. He maintains that structural family therapy has had a substantial influence on his thinking. He takes concepts from family therapy and applies them to organizations, believing that they are helpful in understanding human dynamics in organizations. One example is the family therapy concept of "the loving intention behind a symptom that appears in the system." In applying the concept to organizations, Shandler looks at organizational symptoms and asks the questions: What is the underlying thing that this symptom is pointing to? And what kind of change is it suggesting? Of all the ideas Shandler talks about, the one he regards as most important is intuition. He states that intuition is not something that he learned, although it has been trained. Shandler says, "my intuition is my best tool—the tool that I rely on more than anything that I've learned in any book, anywhere."

John Simmons talks about his personal philosophy coming from a lot of different religious traditions and philosophies; he names Christianity, Judaism, Confucianism, and Buddhism. He further states that his philosophy is based on the importance of core values in improving organizational performance. Those core values are honesty, participation, trust, cooperation, fairness and respect for individual differences. Simmons believes that when they are successfully implanted in an organization's culture, the organization is able to empower people to take more control over the direction of the organization by making better decisions. He believes that the incorporation of core values leads to better working conditions, high performance, and a greater opportunity for sustained growth for the organization.

Shirley Stetson-Kessler talks about her training as a psychologist and her identification with Jungian thought. In addition, she has adopted the theories of Carl Rogers and other humanists into her personal philosophy. Stetson-Kessler also states that Gandhi, Buddha, and Christ are among the spiritual leaders who have had an impact on her philosophy.

John Adams says that his philosophy about organizations is based on a "holistic systems theory" that stems from the Systems Dynamics group at MIT (Massachusetts Institute of Technology). According to Adams, before the MIT group came on the scene, most systems theories were snapshots of a system comprised of input, transformation, output, and feedback. The MIT group, however, made longitudinal studies so that one could see the performance of a system over time by looking at the interaction of positive and negative feedback groups. Adams compares the process involved in holistic systems theory to a thermostat. In addition, he makes biological analogies in explaining the concept of holistic systems theory:

What's the limits of growth? How do other feedbacks come in to limit growth? So why isn't the world overrun with flies? Because there are certain things that keep the fly population down—we'd be seven feet deep in flies in about a week if this were not so. Therefore, looking at interacting cause-and-effect variables over a period of time using computers has helped people to think more systemically or what the New Age calls holistically.

Norma Jean Anderson says her philosophy has to do with empowering people to have a vision and work towards the realization of that vision. She believes in the basic worth of the individual and in affirming that worth to the individual. Anderson says its important that we know that we are more than just flesh and bone. We have within us the power to do anything that we can name, and we also have that same potential for achievement in the organizations where we work. So, the height of who we are is manifested within the organization according to the overall objectives and missions we have chosen. Anderson states that the underpinning of Organization Transformation has to do with people visualizing a new organizational form, naming or stating it in a concrete way, and feeling empowered to work toward it. Anderson states, "As far as underlying philosophies go, there are probably a lot of pieces from a lot of places!"

Bartunek discusses what she considers to be both positive and negative aspects of organizations. Bartunek states that organizations are "messy"; that they are composed of all sorts of intriguing interpersonal and intergroup interactions, they have fascinating impacts on their outer world, and they are capable of being turned in on themselves in a way that's detrimental.

Donald Carew believes in organizations being responsible to their larger communities and to their individual members. He says that organizations have a responsibility to contribute, in a positive way, to the community that they're in and to the quality of life of the people working in the organization. They also have a responsibility for delivering quality service. When those things happen, the organization is more growth-oriented and more viable.

Esty believes in what she calls "a systems approach to organizational consulting." A consultant must take all of the organization's systems into consideration, including the hiring and recruiting system, human resource system, reward system, management system, information systems, etc., and look at how those are put together.

Those systems are what you look at and tinker with or change radically in order to make an organization that is not functioning very well more effective. You'd look at the kind of meanings and structures the organization has. The questions I would ask are: How is decision making done? How autonomous are the people? What kind of teamwork do they have? What are the critical issues? What kind of systems aren't working well? I would then help them to develop interventions that addressed, beefed up, or modified those systems. As far as philosophy underlying that, I come out of the tradition of Marv Weisbord. It goes back to Kurt Lewin, who is certainly one of the founding fathers that I identify with.

Finally, Allen Gordon's philosophy about organizations has to do with an organization's "natural transformation process."

I believe, and this is from a spiritual realm, that things are only alive and transforming. Things naturally transform when they're in the flow of life. Transformation is what life is all about. Transformation, like metamorphosis, is natural unless something interferes with it. We put obstacles in place which prevent the natural transformation process. Transformation would happen without things being in the way; because it's dynamic, it's a process, and it's ongoing.

MEANINGS OF OT

Most of the participants use words such as "fundamental shift" and "radical change" in their responses to the question, "What does Organization Transformation Mean to you—i.e., your definition for OT?"

Adams says that "transition" is going from point A to point B and all you have to do is figure out how to get there. On the other hand, with transformation you don't know what point B is in advance. For individuals, transformation is a fundamental shift in how one thinks. With transformation, a person's mind operates in a new way and the individual obtains a bigger, more systemic, holistic perspective.

According to Anderson, transformation involves a fundamental change in the way people think and react. Transformation in an organization is manifested in its new mission, in the way people in the organization look at their mission, their goals and their objectives. Anderson says that Organization Transformation shows up in the impact that the organization has on the world and in the impact that individuals have internally within the system. She believes that the degree to which people take notice of the transformed organization has to do with its fundamental change. In a transformed organization, there is a fundamental change in the desire of individuals to remain part of the system. It is a change in identity to the extent that it makes room for individuals and it opens up a space of previously unknown possibilities for the organization. Anderson states, "When I think about Organizational Transformation, I think of it in a positive way. The opposite of transformation, to me, is triage."

Bartunek says that Organization Transformation is a qualitative, discontinuous change in the way organizations understand themselves, accompanied by changes in strategy, structure, power, norms, scripts, and practically everything else.

Carew emphasizes that Organization Transformation is an extension of Organization Development (OD) based on a different way of thinking about organizations. Carew says, "I think it's on the cutting edge of the OD field. I see the transforming part as a systems change that includes a more spiritual dimension. I wouldn't necessarily use that word 'spiritual' with organizations because it's fuzzy and it causes some people to be anxious." Carew refers to OT as a paradigm shift with regard to the way organizations think about people and the services they are providing. This new way of thinking is more consistent with respecting and valuing individuals. It's like turning the organizational hierarchy upside-down in such a way that the organization becomes more aware of the people who are closest to customers, the public, clients, or guests. Carew believes that Organizational Transformation implies a major shift in the whole organization.

"I think it's probably a more radical process than Organization Development," says Katharine Esty. "I see it as going more to the root of change and transforming systems more completely than more partial efforts would." Esty defines OT as something that is systemic and complete. She states that Organization Transformation carries the connotation that an organization becomes more interested in being the best that it can be and of using the potential of people. Esty further states that a lot of people believe OT has a spiritual side to it. However, she uses the term, OT, to discuss the process of changing organizations dramatically, using a systems approach.

Harrison Owen calls Organization Transformation a radical discontinuous jump from one state to a totally new one. According to Owen:

Transformation may be up or down, it doesn't always have to be up. Organization Transformation is the organizational search for a "different" way to be. It's what happens when, for whatever reason, the organization as a whole has just run out of its potential at a particular level, and that becomes clear to it because the market changes or because the business is dying, or any one of a million different things.

The major differences in definitions of Organization Transformation have to do with whether an organization can transform "negatively" as well as in a "positive" direction, and the degree to which spirituality is emphasized. A compilation of descriptive words and phrases used in the various definitions follow. This aggregation captures a sense of the variety as well as the similarities in the definitions.

Organization Transformation means a fundamental shift; a paradigm shift; a fundamental change; a change in identity; qualitative, discontinuous change; changes in strategy, structure, power, norms, scripts, etc.; goes more to the root of change; it is second-order change; it is third-order change. It is total change; it means to revitalize or rejuvenate totally; it is behavioral and attitudinal change; a change from one state of reality to an alternate state; a change in context, state of consciousness, structure, content and process; a change in organization consciousness in a very dramatic, deep, radical kind of way; change in assumptions beliefs, values, attitudes, and behavior; it is a positive change. It doesn't always have to be up—many times it's down; it is a radical, discontinuous jump from one state to a new one; a bigger, more systemic, holistic perspective; something that is systemic and complete; an organization becoming the best it can be. It is spiritual; it is a Divine creative process; it is the consciousness that we are all really one—we are all tied to the Divine. Organization Transformation means new life; it has to do with organizational culture, myth, ritual, symbol, stories, energy flow; there is an incredible convergence between OT and some of the work in family therapy. It is proactive; it is visioning the future; it is inductive; it is quicker than OD; it is situational; it means greater productivity; it means continually operating at a higher level of functioning; it is high performance—inspired performance. It is an organization's search for a different way to be; it is creating environments that are more open—more inclusive of all people; it means increasing access, becoming more equitable, becoming more humane. It is consistent with respecting and valuing individuals; it is enriching individual lives; it is moving from a hierarchical management culture to a participative culture; it means everyone is expected to both "think" and "do;" it is a growth activity that's non-judgemental; it is a process of "becoming."

Metaphors and Other Descriptors of OT

Most of the participants agreed that Organization Transformation involves radical, fundamental changes in organizational context, structure, and process. The differences expressed around organizations transforming in a positive versus a negative way is also reflected in the responses to the question, "What adjectives, nouns, metaphors, or other descriptors would you use to describe an organization that has been transformed?" In addition, there seemed to be some differences of opinion as to whether transformation starts on an individual versus a systemic level. Reflecting the same approach as was used with the prior question, a compilation of the descriptors follows. These metaphors and other descriptors convey an even deeper sense of the meanings this group of professionals attaches to Organization Transformation.

In a transformed organization, people are deeply involved in work that has a great deal of meaning, everyone has a sense of commitment and ownership. With transformation, people have broad perspectives that go beyond protecting local turf; the organization has a systems view; people are creative, self-determining. The organization has a longer term perspective, there is global thinking, there is versatility in thinking, the organization moves from automatic pilot to choice. There is a better climate; the organization is more flexible, more open, more intriguing to its members, clients, and whomever comes into contact with it. There are more options; it is uplifted; the organization has high energy: transformation can go in a positive or a negative direction, up and down, back and forth. Conflicts are openly dealt with, the organization has a broad sense of the world, it's like metamorphosis. A transformed organization is generative, it is enabling, it is communal. In a transformed organization, people are being utilized to their fullest capabilities, systems are caring as well as effective, there is synergy in a transformed organization, it has creativity, it uses intuition, and there is a high degree of harmony. The organization doesn't act like a hierarchy, although it might have a hierarchical structure; it is like the butterfly and the chrysalis; it is a continually changing state; it is the process of going from one state of being to a totally different state without restrictions. A transformed organization is metaphor, myth, symbol, ritual, vision; it is context, culture, high performance, flow state, managing energy; it is in consonance with vision; a transformed organization has integral health and well-being, and is fully functioning mentally, spiritually, emotionally, physically, socially, technologically, vocationally, financially, and ecosystemically. A transformed organization is a fully functioning team; it is an awareness that we are interconnected; it is fluid energy—it allows energy to flow in and out; it is a far more energetic, spontaneous, lively, fun place to work. It is palpable; it is kinesthetic; it's intuitive and internally experienced; it means dollar-savings, better solutions, and practical results; it's an inspired organization. A transformed organization is beyond form and structure, time and space; it's not so much what they do as how they do it—process. It is palpable spirit; instead of the people playing the instrument, the instrument plays the people or, really, the music plays both. A transformed organization is in a constant process of renewal; it is like the ocean; it is like a butterfly; it is nonlinear; it is evolving; it is capable of adapting to change; it embraces change; it sees diversity as good, as rich, as healthy. A transformed organization means a change from fairly rigid systems that are based on Western assumptions about predictability, stratification, standardization; it is fluid; in a transformed organization, chaos is not a negative; a transformed organization is feminine; it is holistic. In a transformed organization, relationships are more important than tasks, there is inclusion, individuals feel responsible for the success of the whole. In a transformed organization, individual purposes are partially fulfilled through the aspirations, visions, values, and purposes of the organization. A transformed organization means interdependence, it is inspired performance, it is a heightened sense of energy and creativity; people like to come to work in a transformed organization. In a transformed organization, people report that they are doing things that they never thought they could do before.

Why is There Such a Thing as OT?

This is the fourth question on the Interview Guide. Many of the participants noted that the reasons for the emergence of OT had to do with uncontrollable environmental and cultural trends. Several participants said that Organization Transformation is a natural process that has been happening all along. One said that OT is a human construct aimed at controlling change.

John Adams notes that OT emerged because the electronic age has shrunk organizational response-time to the point where hierarchical, traditional organizations can't respond fast enough in a changing situation. Another reason is the globalization of business. Adams recalls staying in Sheraton Hotels all over India:

We saw an Indian woman a few years ago wearing a sari, complete with nose jewelry and the ear connection; very elegant, with Reebok running shoes on, a Marlboro kickbag over her shoulder, and smoking a French cigarette. The globalization that's going on is incredible. So, response-time shrinkage is a major factor and the global blending.

Another reason Adams gives for the emergence of OT is a shifting spiritual consciousness in terms of the idea that "the god-energy" comes through us rather than being something outside of us that we must go searching for. He notes the contributions to this idea of Marilyn Ferguson, a bestselling author, Rupert Sheldrake in biology, David Bohm in physics, Stephen Hawkin in astrophysics, and Ken Wilbur in sociology. All are, according to Adams, giving the same basic message; that we are creating our own reality as we go along and for the sake of our ultimate survival we must learn to do it more consciously. Therefore, while we are moving into this new spiritual consciousness, at the same time the world is getting smaller, and these two forces are combining to bring about organization transformations.

Robert Johnston believes asking the question, "Why is there such a thing as OT?" is analogous to asking, "Why is there a change in the weather?" He contends that the transformation of organizations has been occurring since the beginning of time. All OT purports to do is make transformation a conscious process so that we can now better choose our transformations, or at least control our response to transforming agents that are too big and powerful for us to control.

Similarly, Rollins says that organization transformation was not created by someone who invented the words, "Organization Transformation"; it has been hapening since the world began. Rollins also reveals his suspicions about some negative implications of the OT movement.

My deepest suspicion is that OT is simply a way for people who are in power to maintain power. It is interesting when you look at the people who are leading OT and at the organizations that they're in, particularly the large ones, which are run by white men; are they serious about transformation? My most suspicious side thinks that this concept was invented and has come into vogue as a way for people who are in power to maintain it and to control it. If they can control the definitions and the language, they are going to control the results—one way or another.

The Single Most Distinguishing Aspect of OT

The fifth question in the Interview Guide is "What is the single most distinguishing aspect, objective, or purpose of OT?" This question elicited the widest variety of responses of the five questions in the "Meanings" section. All but one of the fourteen participants responded to the question.

Three of the responses (Bartunek, Carew, and Simmons) had to do with participation of organizational members. Bartunek thinks that one of the primary defining characteristics of OT is "gigantic quantities of conflict between people." It is her feeling that what is actually going on underneath is a conflict of perspectives. Transformation sets up a means by which conflict can be handled, enabling people operating out of different perspectives to keep talking to each other until something new emerges out of their fights. This, in essence, pushes the fights to a different contextual level at which the conflicting perspectives end up being complementary within a larger scheme of things. Therefore, the single most important objective here is related to a dialogue between perspectives: setting up structures that would enable interactions to occur in such a way that something new is created out of the interaction—something that would never have been dreamed of otherwise. Donald Carew believes that the most significant aspect of OT is that of involving people in decisions that affect their lives. People need to be involved and participate in the creative direction of the organization, and not just do what they're told. People need to contribute to the development of the organization and feel a sense of ownership and partnership. Simmons, also, states that the successful empowerment of people at all levels to take more responsibility for the mission of the organization is the single most distinguishing aspect of OT.

Two other responses (by Johnston and Kueppers) seem roughly to correspond to the notion of universal connectedness. According to Johnston, the single most distinguishing aspect, objective or purpose of OT is wrapped up in the assumption that everything and everyone are fundamentally one in the cosmos. There is at foundation no separation among us; separation is an illusion. "After that, everything else is secondary. Kueppers, in the same vein, states that the single most critical thing about OT is getting people to own who they are, put out who they are, and understand that who they are has to do with being connected. We are connected with ourselves, with others, and with the Ultimate—the Creative—the Divine.

The remaining answers address a variety of themes: Anderson talks about "renewal" and making the organization "different." Rollins emphasizes that the most important aspect of OT involves "race and gender" as the "litmus test" for organizations that are in the process of transforming. Adams comments on the uniqueness of OT and its focus on creative choice, and on articulating future states more clearly. Gordon discusses "high energy that you can feel." Ingle talks about "vision, myth, symbol, and values." Owen says, "for me, it's Spirit." Stetson-Kessler believes that organizations do not transform because it is a good thing to do; it happens only because it must in order for the organization to remain solvent. And Shandler thinks that the primary function of OT is to address the needs of clients.

OT VERSUS OD

Two questions are designed to give further insight into how participants make meaning by comparing their definitions and concepts for Organization Transformation with their understanding of Organization Development (OD). The questions are: What is your definition for Organization Development (OD)? And are there differences between OT and OD? If so, what are they? Table 3.2 is a compilation of the contrasting descriptions given by participants.

Adams states that, according to what Burke and Weinstein wrote in the early 1970s, OD is a normative culture change process that involves a clear contract, a diagnostic phase, and then the application of appropriate technology. This can mean social and psychological applications, including conflict management, survey feedback, relationship building, team building, various training technologies and technostructural changes. His experience of how OD is actually practiced is that practitioners are often so far from the power in the organization that they usually don't get an opportunity to even do those things.

They get opportunities to put band-aids on symptoms, to get into the short-term, local, reactive default position of the organization. There's no power in it, so you get to run training courses occasionally, go around and resolve conflicts, facilitate some flare up; it is perhaps practiced more broadly than that in some places, but I see that a lot.

On the other hand, according to Adams, most people that are working with Organization Transformation ideas are outside of organizations and come in at higher levels. They ask the question, "What results do you want?" In contrast, OD people ask "What hurts?" Another way of differentiating OT from OD is that OD practitioners look at what's already happened and ask, "Can we rectify that?" OT people ask, "What is your current reality today,

Table 3.2
Contrasting Descriptions of OD and OT

Organization Development	Organization Transformation
Starts at lower levels	Starts at higher levels
Far from power centers	Close to power centers
Short-term	Long-term
Local perspective	Global perspective
Reactive	Proactive
Problem-solving, deductive	Inductive
"What hurts?" Diagnosis	"What results do you want?" Vision
Realities past-to-present	Present-to-future realities
Make better, improve, make more effective	Make different
Goals, objectives, mission	Vision
Minor changes	Major shift
Piecemeal	Systemic, holistic
Mechanical	Spiritual
Improvement of organization	Empowerment of people

where do you want to get to, and what can we do to reduce the gap?" Also, viewpoints are often "past-to-present" for OD professionals and "present-to-future" for OT practitioners. Adams acknowledges that there is a lot of overlap between OT and OD and that boundaries are not that clear-cut. He believes that there needn't be any differences between OT and OD.

Anderson states that Organization Development means taking an organization as is and making it more effective through training, consulting, certain technostructural changes, education, the hiring of new people, etc. However, the organization maintains the same mission, goals and objectives. OD makes the organization better by fixing something; however, it maintains the same identity. In contrast, Organization Transformation means that the organization becomes a different entity. Like Adams,

Anderson acknowledges that OD and OT practitioners may do some of the same things; however, OT involves a broader leap in the mind. The developer thinks, "How can I make the organization more effective?" Whereas the OT practitioner thinks, "How can I visualize this organization so that it serves the world in a new way." Owen, like Anderson, says that Organization Development is making an organization better, whereas Organization Transformation is essentially making it different.

According to Simmons, Organization Development involves an effort to bring about improvements, but not necessarily empowerment or full participative management. OT is genuine empowerment. OD is often done by management for management without other employee concerns being given any kind of equal weight.

Bartunek says that OD is planned organizational change which involves collaboration between a consultant and organizational members. It takes a while, uses social science principles, and is action-research based (which is a diagnostic approach). Transformation cannot typically happen using OD methods. If you take a diagnostic approach to problems, you can't see the problems from a perspective that is radically different from the normal ones. So, with OD the organization is "stuck" on making improvements within the already accepted framework. According to Bartunek, for transformation to occur there has to be a crisis that cannot be dealt with by using the usual framework for making sense of things. OT calls for an alternative vision of the organization.

Ingle defines OD as a broad category of change-agent activities aimed at improving the performance of organizations, but many times performance ends up being defined rather narrowly. On the other hand, OT places attention on myth, ritual, symbol, culture, the stories within the organization, and the next level up is vision. Ingle states that OD practitioners talk about goals and objectives and sometimes mission; however, you rarely hear OD people talk about vision. "It's clear that when we look at effective organizations and vital organizations, vision is there."

Johnston says OD predominantly helps organizations to solve their problems. Johnston believes that there are exceptions with some OD practitioners, but most are more deductive and problem-solving in their reasoning, reactive and piecemeal in their orientations when they go in to help organizations. OD practitioners, on the whole, are not concerned about overall systems change. OT, in contrast, is inductive, proactive, quicker, and systemic. It involves a change in organization consciousness in a very dramatic, radical kind of way.

William Kueppers says that OD involves a consciousness within organizations of a need to develop people so that they acquire the skills to do the tasks that are needed as the organization evolves; it looks at the skill level and the professional development level of players within the organization. The OT practitioner brings in a spiritual overlay. OT practitioners work with skills and knowledge, and tries to move the organization into a more expanded consciousness of all people's interconnectedness. Kueppers states that he is not sure if one would be able to tell OD and OT practitioners apart easily because the difference has to do with the type of consciousness they bring to the organization.

Rollins also believes that in a lot of ways OD is not significantly different from Organization Transformation. However, he views OD as more mechanical. One way to think about OD, according to Rollins, is that it is the methodology, techniques, and tools by which you might achieve transformation. Transformation, on the other hand, is spiritual. There is a different sense of the results that occur in the organization when a transformational process is involved: a basic sense of renewed spirit, and a deeper sense of organizational members being committed to each other. Transformation literally means a deeper, more fundamental change.

OT'ers

Many of the participants mention that they don't necessarily enjoy making comparisons between OD and OT. They see both as useful, although they may be different. The next set of questions attempts to go back to a singular focus on Organization Transformation. However, that shift in focus was difficult for many participants to make after the comparisons between OD and OT were made.

Question number nine on the Interview Guide, "What distinguishes an OT practitioner/theorist from other organizational practitioners's theorists?", was eliminated after the first three interviews. It seemed redundant and solicited no new information. Question number twelve, "How do you fit into this picture?", was also eliminated because, after the respondents answered the other questions, the answer to twelve was quite obvious.

The remaining questions brought some interesting responses. They are: On what points do OT'ers agree? And, on what points do OT'ers disagree? Table 3.3 summarizes all of the responses to these questions. The table is simply a compilation of the responses. That is to say, not every participant agreed with every response represented. However, several similar responses

Table 3.3
On What Points Do OT'ers Agree/Disagree?

Agreement	Disagreement
We don't have a choice; it's for the planet's survival	Theory
Basic human rights are sacred	Methodologies, approaches philosophies
OT'ers are healers of a sort	The process of education/ influencing young people
There is no one "right" way	
Human development is good	Issues of nationalism vs. universal group/nation
Empowerment of people vital	Vocabulary, various shades of meaning
Our interconnection, oneness	
Basic ecological interconnection of all systems	Variations on the central theme of our oneness
OT is fundamental change	How to bring about transformation
Direction of change toward more humanistic values	Forms of interventions
	Roles practitioner plays
Conceptually the importance of race and gender issues	Technology and tools
OT is quantum leap into something we don't fully understand	Length of time that it takes to transform
OT is exciting--on the cutting edge	Specific strategies and techniques
Creativity, empowerment, self-determination are important	
We're just scratching the surface of what people can do	
Transformation causes something that is qualitatively different than before	
Transformative changes have multiple dimensions	
Organizational structure should be fluid/dynamic	

were given by different participants. To the question, "On what points do OT'ers agree?", several participants answered: fundamental organizational change; empowerment of organizational members; and human and systemic interconnections. To the question, "On what points do OT'ers disagree?", many participants noted that they would disagree about the "how to's," that is, the methods, approaches, strategies, and techniques for facilitating Organization Transformation.

Expressing doubt about OT'ers having much in common that would make them a cohesive group of theorists and practitioners, Bartunek believes that OT'ers would probably agree that the organization is qualitatively different after transformation has occurred; and they might agree that the thing that changes has multiple dimensions. However, OT'ers would probably disagree on many more things. Bartunek says "OT people talk about entirely different mindsets of stuff. I'm not even sure we'd be using the same terms for most of the stuff, so we wouldn't even know whether we agree or disagree."

Similarly, Ingle says,

This is not a group that can be put in a box. There is a collection of individuals who sort of trail off in really far-out dimensions. What would they agree on? The feeling is that it sometimes gets written up as if this is already a field, but in reality it is not. There are people who are doing this, but it's an area of exploration, and most of the people that are involved in it came out of OD, and have strong OD backgrounds. There are also folks from more spiritually inclined dimensions and there are other types of visionaries. But clearly, it's an area of exploration. I think the OTers would agree that transformation requires a certain level of personal development and exploration for one to be comfortable and competent doing it. What else do they agree on? I have trouble going beyond that, because there are lots of differences as well. I think OTers would disagree about specific strategies and techniques. And you can get tension between the more spiritually inclined—the folks who want to talk about the spirit and work-spirit versus folks who are still more in an OD mode—more instrumental, thinking structurally. There are differences because it's an area of exploration, and the book has not been written and probably won't be for a while. There are differences about how actually to pull things off, but OT is an area of mutual exploration.

CONCLUSIONS: AN ONTOLOGICAL FRAMEWORK

Themes consist of metaphors, symbols, and other descriptions of Organization Transformation that occur in the data. More specifically, the data were searched for the following:

- Adjectives that were used in reference to Organization Transformation to express the quality of the phenomenon or something attributed to it.

- Nouns that were used in place of Organization Transformation to further explain what it is and how it works.

- Metaphors that were used to transfer to the words, "Organization Transformation," the sense and meanings of other words; metaphors imply comparisons that are primarily used to apply the meanings of other words to the phenomenon Organization Transformation.

Approximately 1,875 themes were identified in the raw data. The themes were categorized and analyzed using a four-part ontological schema developed by the researcher.

This ontological schema is a model or conceptual framework through which one can make sense out of the data. As with all such models, it focuses and frames the data in a particular way so that they may be discussed in an understandable, shorthand manner. The researcher recognizes that there are perhaps an infinite number of models that may be developed to explain and describe the data. However, this conceptual framework seemingly emerged out of the findings, and was the only framework known to the researcher that adequately explained all of the themes that were identified. Other schemes were tested for their applicability to the themes; for example, Burrell and Morgan's "Sociological Paradigms" (1979) initially seemed most applicable, but later proved inadequate because it did not explain most of the data.

The ontological famework developed by the present researcher, based on Johnston's (1985) third-order change perspective, greatly aided the inductive analytical process necessary to summarize and interpret the large numbers of themes identified. The four categories within this conceptual framework (see Figure 3.1) are as follows:

Figure 3.1
An Ontological Framework for Categorizing Themes

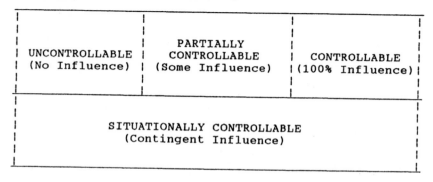

- *Uncontrollable.* These themes are nomothetic in nature, and are characterized by intractable natural law or principle. They may also be described as deterministic, providential, fatalistic, or transpersonal, and are characteristics that defy human control or influence.
- *Partially Controllable.* These are interactive themes that primarily deal with human interactions that are systemic and/or interpersonal. They are characterized by their ability to be influenced, but not totally controlled.
- *Controllable.* These are ideographic themes that focus on the individual's ability to choose and control. These individualistic themes may also be described as humanistic, independent, even counterdependent. In effect they say that humans create and totally control their own realities.
- *Situationally Controllable.* Themes that recognize the existence of all three of the above are labelled "situational." They imply that humans have control, partial control, and no control in different situations. They may also embrace opposites and be described as simultaneous dichotomies or companionable polarities.

Table 3.4 summarizes the findings. The table was compiled based on a selection of the themes from the raw data, which included many descriptors. Many of the themes were recurring and the selections were checked for duplications. The sample was taken from the larger list which was compiled from the raw data; that list contains approximately 1,875 themes, including duplications.

Several important phrases that occur repeatedly, but are not listed in Table 3.4 because they apply to more than one of the four categories are:

- Fundamental change
- Qualitative discontinuous change
- Second-order change, and
- Major paradigm shift.

These concepts are explanations for the phenomenon of Organization Transformation and may be thought of as synonyms.

Based on my interpretation of the context in which the participants in this study used these themes, it seems clear to me that it would be possible to describe participants as having basic assumptions about their interventions that could be characterized as either uncontrollable, partially controllable, controllable, or situationally controllable. However, this study categorizes themes and not the participants because they were not specifically questioned about their ontological assumptions. Without more specific data, it may be misleading to make any more definitive judgments than the general ones made here.

Table 3.4
Themes, Metaphors, and Other Descriptors Categorized by Ontological Assumptions

Un-controllable	Partially Controllable	Controllable	Situationally Controllable
Ocean	Co-create	Free choice	Triune rela-tionship
Flow	Collaborate	100% re-sponsible	Spiritual
Ecosystemic	Community	Create	Holographic
Butterfly	Synergy	Visioning	Embraces op-posites
Spirit	Systemic in-teractions	Free space	Oneness
Metamorphose	Inclusion	Reform	Flexible
Adaptive	Connected-ness	Ownership	Versatility
Threatening		Self-deter-mining	More options
React	Goals	Empowered	Holistic
Chrysalis	Cooperation	Planned change	Parallel processes
Organism	System of people	In-outward thing	Broad Per-spectives
Ongoing pro-cess	People dis-agree	Producing results	Global
Sense of Crisis	Conflict	Directing	Systemic and complete
Spiritual law	Egalitarian	Enabling	Appropriate structure
Letting go	Love	Decisions	Balanced
Programmed	Multi-cultural	Authentic	Integral
Sea of Mind energy	Social	Self-suf-ficient	Third-order change
Divine pro-cess	"We"		

What the data in Table 3.4 suggest is the importance of Organization Transformation practitioners examining their assumptions about the potential controllability of any change project that they undertake. If it is assumed that the consultant or client has complete control over the outcomes and, in fact, the situation is fraught with variables too big or complex, the change effort is doomed to failure. On the other hand, if it is assumed that "the fates will out" and the practitioner resigns him/herself to blowing with the wind, he or she will undoubtedly fail to live up to the potential for managing the project.

4

Consequences/Applicability

Participant responses to five questions are discussed in this chapter:

- What impact has OT had? (I.e., what are the contributions of OT?)
- What future impact do you predict that OT will have?
- What are the current and possible future resistances to OT? From whom?
- Is OT more applicable to certain types of domains and not applicable to others? Explain.
- What are the potentials of OT given our current social, economic, and political systems?

When questioned concerning the current impact of OT, many of the participants also responded to the next question concerning the future impact of OT. For that reason, the two questions are discussed together. In addition, the question: "What are the potentials of OT given our current social, economic, and political systems?" seemed redundant given several participants' answers to the question: "Is OT more applicable to certain types of domains and not applicable to others?"; those participants were not asked the last question.

IMPACT/CONTRIBUTIONS OF OT

Again, two questions that are discussed together in this section:

- What impact has OT had? (I.e., what are the contributions of OT?)
- What future impact do you predict that OT will have?

Many participants express the belief that the impact of Organization Transformation thus far has been small; others say that the impact is currently negligible, but growing; at least one participant believes that the future impact may be insignificant; and yet others believe that the future impact will be great.

Although Michael Shandler says that the overall impact of Organization Transformation is negligible, he gives examples of the impact of OT on specific organizations with which he has worked.

OT has had no real impact on organizations in general. But, I can name specific organizations, even very conventional ones, where Organization Transformation technologies have absolutely transformed the way those people go about their daily lives. For example, Armco Eastern Steel Division in Middletown, Ohio, has radically transformed the way they think and do business as a result of our Organization Transformation efforts. AM International, another example, is in the process of radically changing—all the way from the top; it hasn't started filtering down yet, but it soon will. A small company, Campdell Hausfeld, the world's largest manufacturer of air compressors (they make compressors for Sears' Craftsman labels and others) have been profoundly influenced by my OT efforts. There's a part of Columbia University that I worked with that has been influenced incredibly by creating a vision and working with their vision. There is a large telecommunications business, Contel, that has been influenced. So, if you look at the whole world, OT is a very young field and there has been relatively little impact; but then in the same breath I want to make sure that I honor and acknowledge not only my efforts, but the efforts of a lot of other people who are doing what I call Organization Transformation work—they are having an impact. But it's like trying to wear a thread against a big rock; you can eventually wear the rock down, but it's going to take a hell of a long time.

Shandler's comments when asked specifically about the future impact of Organization Transformation seemed a bit more hopeful than his previous statement reveals; he thinks OT ideas are going to creep in increasingly. They are influencing the OD Network, for example. According to Shandler, OT will need to become much more sophisticated than it is now before it gains greater credibility, but some of the thinking in OT is the most courageous in the field in that it deals with the leading edge of the latest thinking in biology, human systems thinking, and physics.

John Adams also says that OT has not had a widespread impact on organizations; however, he talks about transformation having a significant impact on individuals. Adams believes that although OT has not impacted very many corporations or communities yet, there are a few cases. According to Adams, the primary impact of OT thus far has been to legitimize a lot of people who have been thinking about transformation, but didn't think it was OK to talk about it. When they recognize each other, they can get together for support and that gives them the inspiration to go on and be more explicit about it. Looking to the future, Adams predicted that Organization Transformation will become a part of the "mainstream way of life." He says that OT will probably go through the same sort of life cycle as OD—through a missionary phase, then through a technician phase, and then will become more of an integrated, mainstream phenomenon, which is therefore "normal development." In other words, Adams believes that this is the course of all practice—to become a stable part of the status quo. However, he believes that there will always be people who are mavericks, "chomping away at the front end" and being on the leading edge. Although Adams states that he does not know what the future holds for OT, he thinks the best of all possible outcomes would be that it will turn around the chaotic situation that organizations are in today over the next twenty or thirty years. If this happens, Adams believes that organizations would promote individual equity and they would have sustainable appropriate technology in science—appropriate technology meaning that "better living through chemistry would go the way of all bad ideas; we wouldn't be creating so many toxic chemicals and then dumping them in the field out behind the plant." Appropriate also means that we would learn to live as a global community in a way that is ecologically sound, and that organizations will exist for the benefit of the people in them as well as in order to make a profit.

Anderson is also among those who feel that Organization Transformation has not yet had a significant impact. She states that the future of OT is dependent on the numbers of people who are willing to join the effort. According to Anderson, there are only a few people who dare to even talk about it because transformation has been identified with spiritual work. "Even though people want their organizations to be transformed, they are waiting on other people to say it first; in psychology, they call that pluralistic ignorance." Anderson believes that, if we could in some way check it out, we would find that many people are thinking in terms of Organization Transformation. Recently, quite a few people have decided to write about it, give workshops on it, and talk with their peers about it.

According to Anderson, what the future holds will depend on how many people will decide to speak out and say: "This is what I'm about," and know it is legitimate, practice it, and share it with others.

Bartunek's response has to do with her belief in the difficulty and painfulness of the transformation process. She lays out a bleak scenario: within a few companies, quietly, the notion of Organization Transformation is really successful. Then somebody popularizes it and every organization rushes to announce that it is going through a transformation and then nothing else will happen.

I believe that if OT really happens, it's not easy, it's not a lot of fun, it takes a long time, it involves a wrenching change in perspectives that can be great in the long run, but isn't fun for a lot of people while they're going through it, and people don't want to do it. The ideal impact would be that it would happen in situations where it needs to happen and that people will have an appreciation that you can't just announce that it's there and it'll happen.

Katharine Esty talked about how OT has "infiltrated" organizations in an indirect, covert manner. "I certainly don't think that people in Fortune 500 companies know that term, OT; but I think that interests have switched and now the language has changed." Esty states that consultants now talk about things that were previously not in their discussions. They are much more apt to use words like love, work-spirit, meaning, extraordinary teams, and organizations reaching their highest potential. Esty believes that OT has transformed how people think about organizations. "I think it's been more like seeping, infiltrating into people's consciousness indirectly." As for future impact, Esty thinks that because people are interested in how a global community will work, OT is going to be increasingly important. In the future, she sees an increasing infiltration of OT ideas and concepts until the critical mass of people is thinking about those kinds of issues.

Bill Kueppers discusses the current impact of Organization Transformation on individuals. He belongs to an organization called Renaissance Business Associates, which in his estimation is essentially an Organization Transformation Network:

They operate out of a deep sense of character; they call it "deepest quality of character." What is happening is that more of these types of organizations exist. People are taking greater ownership for who they are, and are expressing different ways of being within organizations, which is refreshing. Other people see it and are magnetized to it because it is refreshing—it's spirited.

Kueppers believes that organizations are becoming more exciting places to work as a result of transformations. He also believes that the numbers of people who are going into business for themselves has something to do with it. He feels that the trend toward independent entrepreneurships where people are picked up by organizations on an ad hoc basis is a healthy sign. Like Bartunek, Kueppers talks about the painfulness of the OT process. He believes that organizations are becoming far more productive and leaner, but not necessarily "meaner." In the short term, it is very painful for a lot of people, primarily those who haven't taken ownership for themselves. Yet, in contrast, he seems sure that people will begin to look forward to continual personal transformations.

We're moving, but we're not there yet. There are a lot of people who are still looking to organizations for paternalistic care rather than looking at what they bring to the organization, and if it's a good fit. Initially, we're going to have a lot of anguish as people feel the pain. As organizations become leaner, people will be about in the streets for a while and will start to find healthy niches. People won't continue doing the same thing forever. As their lives progress, they'll be going through their own personal transformations; going into their cocoons and saying, "What's next?"

Harrison Owen, like Esty, discussed the impact of Organization Transformation on language and how it is becoming more acceptable. Owens believes that there is a deepening awareness of the reality of transformation in our lives. We have begun to create some useful ways of dealing with the phenomenon of Organization Transformation. One "hard impact" is that there is now a literature on OT.

The New York Times writes about it; *Fortune* magazine writes about it. Eight years ago, if you said "culture," as we did, somebody in the executive suite would think you were selling opera tickets. Today you can't pick up a book, even standard mainline books, without somebody talking about organizational culture—the language is coming into play. Can you imagine the corporation that doesn't actually feel guilty about not having a vision statement? They may have no idea what vision is; but, that's all right. I would be surprised if you find an issue of *The Wall Street Journal* or *Barron's* that doesn't mention transformation; "The company was transformed, the culture was transformed." So I think we see the impact. Five years ago, I thought it would be a nice idea to take one hundred people and let them know nothing more than who is coming to a conference, when it starts, and when it's over—and say, with varying levels of probability, "You're gonna have a successful conference." I still don't have any problem with it at this juncture; I don't even feel any compulsion to try to prove it to them—I just do it.

Simmons' view was that, although Organization Transformation has had a positive affect on some organizations, its future economic impact on organizations in this country will be poor due to the current leadership in industry and government. However, according to Simmons, a major contribution of OT has been helping organizations to survive in our economy and helping them to compete internationally. He believes that where OT *has* been effective, it has made the difference between life and death for certain companies. It has also had the effect of changing peoples lives at work. People now see that they can have a friendly, cooperative work environment, rather than an authoritarian, competitive one. Simmons believes that OT could make the difference in the efforts of U.S. companies to retain their economic status. "So, it has a big job to do, and I think there is no other way that we're even going to retain our current second-class status unless we extend OT to a lot of larger and medium-size organizations." Simmons states that the U.S. has fallen to second class because of our external trade deficit, uncontrolled inflation, and poor-quality products: "you pick twenty parameters and we're second-class compared to the Japanese, and Swedes, and West Germans." He believes that part of it has to do with the poor quality of our training and education. Simmons believes that if a significant number of organizations in this country were to transform, we would be able to compete more effectively with the top three countries. However, he is not optimistic that this will happen, because national and corporate leaders are not aware of the existing problems. "I think Organization Transformation is going to grow significantly over the next couple of decades, but I don't think it's going to have the economic impact that it should have; and that's not a reflection on Organizational Transformation, but rather on the environment we are in."

Stetson-Kessler, like others, alludes to OT being a painful process; however, her metaphor for OT was "a little seed that's just beginning to sprout." Stetson-Kessler believes that OT is just beginning to make a difference and how much of one all depends on what organizations you examine. She says that OT has made a huge difference so far for those few organizations who are aware. Although OT is in the beginning stages of its development into a field, Stetson-Kessler thinks that in the future there will be a huge explosion of growth and probably a lot of turmoil and chaos. She says the idea is frightening to people. The impact of Organization Transformation will be tempered by the extent to which people can let go of those fears.

Carew talks about OT being a cultural movement that some Organization Transformation people are attempting to lead. He believes that the OT movement is a reflection of what is happening in the world.

Naisbitt said that leadership is finding a parade and getting in front of it; OT people are getting in front of a parade that's happening anyway. I think that they will provide some impetus, some spirit, some different ways of thinking. A lot of them are writing about it and are like "goosing" agents.

Allen Gordon discusses the personal impact of transformation on individuals, who in turn impact organizations and societies.

I think that OT has had tremendous impact on individuals. I've seen it happen most in certain spiritual people and spiritual organizations. The contributions of OT to the realm of organizations will bring a breath of fresh air; it will bring about the possibility for true health in organizations. I think the future impact is going to be great. I don't believe that organizations are independent from individuals and families, nations and societies; the impact of transformation on individuals is likely to spill over—it can't help but spill over if it's true transformation.

Johnston discusses Organization Transformation and Organization Development as being complementary fields of theory and practice. He believes that OT is causing a major paradigm change in the field of OD. OT is putting a broader, more viable, holographic foundation under OD than existed previously. "I expect, as OT and OD together as a synergistic pair mature, we'll see a lot more effectiveness resulting from our efforts with organizations." Johnston states that there are some question marks, uncertainties and dubious feelings about traditional OD; people are asking, "Is OD really doing anything?" He sees OT as something dramatically different, although it appears to have grown out of OD.

Bryant Rollins talks about the fundamental impact of people of color and women on the transformation of organizations.

There has been enormous changes in organizations because of the presence of women and people of color in those systems, but we have yet to bring that up to a conscious awareness. For example, the book *Mumbo Jumbo* talks about the effect of African Americans in American society at a very subliminal level. We are the freeing, unpredictable, wild influence; jazz just didn't come from nowhere, neither did gospel. In many ways, we've had a fundamental effect on the West; not superficial, but fundamental. That impact has been in the culture and now it's moving into institutions, because we're moving into institutions. So the changes are deep and fundamental and we're just starting to acknowledge them.

OT, according to Grant Ingle, is increasingly having impact; myth, ritual, symbol, vision are powerful variables and have probably been discovered before. "We're just rediscovering them." Ingle says that OT has a rebelliousness about it which perhaps flows from the rebelliousness of the 1960s. Grant Ingle also acknowledges the need for a "multicultural imperative" in the Organization Transformation movement. He says that, without such an imperative, OT will have a limited impact.

My concern is that it's predominantly a white activity and until we figure out a way to bridge OT with a multicultural imperative, I think it's going to be of limited impact. Therein lies OT's real strength and I'm still struggling with trying to figure out how to build that bridge. My personal vision is that OT will involve a very powerful integration of multiculturalism as a key part. We talk about an increasingly multicultural world and increasingly multicultural organizations, we're going to have to pay particular attention to ourselves. The major question is how do we create organizations that mainstream lots of different energies and still respect differences?

RESISTANCES TO OT

What are the current and possible future resistances to OT? From whom? Participants' responses to these questions acknowledged that current and future resistances to OT come from individuals, groups, and organizations; but primarily from individuals. The most common theme found in the responses is fear—individual fear of the unknown, as Rollins noted in his response:

The resistances have to do with fear of the unknown. I think that everybody experiences fear. Even people who are involved in organizational change, myself included, have fears regarding the consequences of those changes. The people who go ahead in spite of their fear and do what they think is right are the people who become the drivers of transformation.

Anderson also talks about individual fear of the unknown being the primary cause of resistance to Organization Transformation. According to Anderson, the resistance comes from people thinking that they are safe or secure, not daring to go for the unknown and being afraid of it. There is a natural death in transformation, and even though some people are having a hard time, they would prefer to stay with that hard time out of fear, rather than face the death and rebirth of transformation.

Likewise, Stetson-Kessler points to fear as the main cause of resistance. However, she specifically points to fearfulness by those with power, namely white males, as the primary deterrent to Organization Transformation.

We work with groups all the way from high-tech companies like Digital Equipment Corporation to a highly militaristic former Bell System group, which is a large client. It doesn't much matter which system we're in, when things get to the point of shaking the foundations, people who know themselves are wide open to the possibility of tranformation, while people who don't freeze in fear—I see it happening. To the extent that you could generalize around the pockets of people who are most likely to be afraid, I'd say white males, definitely. People of color and women are much more flexible. Flexibility has been their history—"So, yeah, what else is new?" Those groups are much more prepared for the whole possibility of what the next century will bring. Fortunately, they're going to be the largest numbers. I'd like to find a way to let those who appear to have the power of the pocketbook know that they don't have to be afraid. However, the only way to do that is by helping them to know themselves, and that's a scary route.

Kueppers talks about individual resistances that happen as a result of transformation being forced on organizations. Many individuals want to be taken care of by organizations, and the reaction is dramatic when organizations can no longer do that because of survival needs. More and more organizations are going to force people to take ownership for themselves, according to Kueppers, and the resistances are going to come from displaced individuals.

Owen discusses a possible massive backlash of people attempting to control their continually transforming organizations.

Organizations are increasingly going to see that structure always has to be appropriate for the spirit, particularly in the kind of economic world we're moving into. Instead of feeling anxious and guilty every time they reorganize, they'll understand that they'll probably have five or six different organizational structures going simultaneously. There could be a massive backlash as people try to control their world, and if they do we will end the world. People don't like to lose control.

Shandler's response to the question has to do with the ability of OT practitioners to "honor" and manage resistances. Shandler sees resistance as a natural part of people's basic mind-sets. He believes that OT practitioners have to become a lot more sophisticated in how they present themselves because a lot of the resistance has to do with OT practioners not taking into consideration that people have mind-sets, and that they have resistances.

OT, so far, has not worked appropriately with resistance; it doesn't know how to honor resistance. OT practitioners need to learn appropriate attitudes and forms to join more with their clients; where the clients are rather than where they wish they would be.

Adams says that the identification with money and power is the primary cause for resistance to Organization Transformation. This is exemplified by the bumper sticker which reads: "The one who dies with the most toys wins." He believes that the accumulation of money and power is still the driving force for a critical mass of people in the United States. "As long as there's an attachment to money and power, then the principles we stand for will face difficulties."

Bartunek discusses how fads tend to undercut the power of a movement such as Organization Transformation. Her image of what might happen is that people will say, "If you're an organization that hasn't been transformed, then what good are you?" So, organizations will do a few superficial things and then announce that they are about something broader than they use to be, thus polluting the whole movement. Her hope is that if this happens someone will figure out what the underlying values are and will come up with a new word for it that may enable it to continue—but it'll have to continue under a new label.

Esty says that resistances to Organization Transformation come from a rational linear mind-set that is primarily masculine, and that OT tends to be more feminine. Many people in organizations object to "new-age" types of activities as "soft," that they are not rational, not linear. Esty believes that people are still very concerned with the rational; at the same time, they are aware that there's more.

A lot of the OT values are what have been traditionally connected with the feminine; cooperation, caring, spirituality, values of the heart—things that have also been associated with women. I think that there's a resistance to anything that seems soft and fluffy; but there is also an openness to it—so it's not resistances across the board. The resistance comes primarily from the kind of people who have been trained in professions such as engineering.

Gordon says that resistance comes primarily from people who want something more concrete to "grasp." OT seems to be a nebulous concept difficult for many people to understand, especially those who rely heavily on structure, regulations and rules. People don't really need a lot of structure, according to Gordon; however, those people who believe structure is absolutely necessary are those who resist OT because it is contrary to their view of the world. The resistance then is not from any particular group of people, but from everywhere. Gordon sums up the attitude by saying, We've done it this way, for many years, down the line, so forget about this loosey-goosey transformation synergistic stuff!"

Grant Ingle, like Stetson-Kessler, describes the primary barrier as coming from white males.

Being white and male tends to be a barrier. I think that OT practitioners need to do a lot of personal work around multicultural issues. There's a tendency for consultants not to see that and that's a problem. Until OT starts addressing multicultural issues it won't draw people of color. We need those folks sitting in the small groups. Through diversity we can find new routes to synergy. For me that's a really exciting vision—multicultural and multinational discussions with people from around the world about Organization Transformation.

APPLICABILITY OF OT

Is OT more applicable to any particular domain as opposed to any other? That is question number eighteen on the Interview Guide. Of the eleven participants who answered this question, seven said no—OT is not more applicable to any particular domain as opposed to any other; three said yes, OT appears to be more amenable in certain types of organizations; and one said that the answer is both yes and no—that all organizations could benefit by OT, but some are more receptive than others.

Esty, Adams, and Bartunek answered "yes" to the question. Esty believes that there are some types of industries more receptive to OT than others. Although she says it is not that clear-cut, "old-line" manufacturing firms are probably the least favorable soil for OT and younger high-tech firms are more flexible and would be more likely to make room for OT. Adams also agrees that OT might catch on faster in a young high-tech organization because the entrepreneurial spirit is not too different from the transformational spirit. Also a lot of change is part of reality for high-technology organizations: "It's not like you're coming in and trying to change something that's had years and generations to settle into a way of being— you've got something that's already in flux." According to Adams, those stable, assembly-line production organizations are probably less interested in vision and more interested in maintaining the status quo. Bartunek thinks that OT is perhaps more applicable to particular types or forms of organizations than others, but she is not quite sure what the meaningful characteristics are yet. She guesses that the meaningful organizational characteristics would have to do with the patterns that are set up for handling conflict.

Gordon, Anderson, Carew, Owen, Rollins, Simmons, and Stetson-Kessler responded "no" to the question. They say that Organization Transformation is equally applicable to all kinds of organizations. Gordon states that OT has to be applicable to all organizations, or it can't be applicable to any. "If that's not the way it works, then what you're calling OT is not OT because OT is a process, not a picture." Carew also believes that any organization would be enhanced by moving in the direction of transformation; whether it's a small construction firm, a major manufacturing organization, or a Fortune 500 company. "From a mom-and-pop store to a great conglomerate—I think that all of them can move in the direction of transformation; where people are working with people rather than for people."

Michael Shandler answers both "yes" and "no" to the question about the applicability of OT to particular domains. His comments are the opposite of comments made by some who answered "yes" to the question.

The short answer is no—organizations are organizations are organizations. However, there are some organizations that are more receptive than others. The interesting thing is that the types of organizations calling me in are traditional organizations that are under pressure from overseas competition. They know that they have to do something different. They know it in their bones, or they're going to go out of business. I work with a lot of steel companies and paper companies—these are traditional smokestack industries that know they have to think differently, or the Japanese or the Philippines, or some organization someplace else is going to be supplying. My experience has been that the high-tech industries are so aloof and so super-sophisticated that they are very often not open. Whereas, some of the organizations out in the Midwest are more open because they're less sophisticated, they haven't been exposed to so much, they're not so spoiled, and they get things a lot faster.

POTENTIALS OF OT

Question 19 is the last question in the "Consequences/Applicability" section of the Interview Guide. It provides a good summary of the participant's views about OT's palpability in our current environment. The question is, "What are the potentials of OT given our current, social, economic, and political systems? The tone of the responses to this question is mixed. Some participants seem very optimistic about the potential of Organization Transformation's impact on the current environment, and others are quite pessimistic. For example, John Adams states:

You can't just look at the political situation in one country. Also, if the economic problems and the environmental problems come home to roost in the next couple of years, then there will be lots of transformations, lots of violence, lots of fires, and lots of problems; and who knows which ideology is going to prevail. I would suggest that probably a charismatic authoritarian would prevail because, when people are in a short-term local reactive mode, they tend to look to somebody to solve their problems for them. So, if somebody can capture the moment by saying "I can solve your problems," they'll gets lots of support. I'm not very optimistic in terms of the political situation. In the short term, I'm pessimistic; however, in the long term I'm very optimistic. I think maybe we need to go through a kind of a cleansing, a phoenix move to get to the other side. If that's what it takes, then I guess that's what we'll do.

Like Adams, Jean Bartunek paints a not-so-pretty picture of the future. She believes that in some ways there are large numbers of transformations going on that aren't happening in the way OT people like to talk about them.

Some are partly the result of mergers and acquisitions being such a fashionable thing to do. Those types of changes end up being by definition transformations, changing organizations' understandings of themselves. In this case, because somebody purchased them who says, "Well, you're different now." I think the political and economic and social situation in the country right now is extremely conducive to that kind of situation and absolutely not at all to my ideal of a desirable transformation; that is in part because it takes a while. So, I'm talking about a mass negative transformation happening in most organizations, with a few people getting real rich from it and lots of people losing.

Esty's outlook is also glum, but hopeful. She believes that the economy is probably going to turn sour primarily due to our inability to handle the competition overseas. She believes that, as companies go through their "lean and mean" stages, people will gradually become more open to Organization Transformation.

On the other hand, Norma Jean Anderson is very optimistic about the potentials of OT in the current environment. She believes that OT has high potentials and that social, economic, and even political systems can be transformed. Recent occurrences all over the world seem to be supporting Anderson's beliefs. Like Anderson, Gordon also has a very positive outlook for the future of Organization Transformation. He believes that OT's potentials are unlimited and "all-embracing."

In his response to the question, Kueppers points out some healthy economic, social, and political trends which he connects to Organization Transformation.

I think it's no accident that Russia and the United States are more closely looking at a healthy relationship. I don't think it's anything apart from what OT is about. We're seeing ourselves as connected, more and more. The Armenian earthquake is a perfect example. Do you think the United States reached out because we were enemies? People reached out in the United States because people saw our connectedness to the human community. They showed the suffering on American TV. So, economically, politically and socially we're beginning to see a connectedness. What you're seeing is fear beginning to take it's first veil down. As the world becomes smaller, we begin to see our oneness, our unity—no matter what country it is or our difficulties with them. So, I see that OT has all sort of implications, and it gets played out in politics and in economics both within the United States and globally.

Shandler's outlook for Organization Transformation was primarily positive. He believes that OT has "terrific potential." However, to realize that potential, OT must learn to "join clients where they are, not where we would like them to be." Stetson-Kessler was likewise optimistic in her view of the potentialities of Organization Transformation. She says, "I think the doors and windows are wide open and the possibilities are absolute." She believes that although the outlook seems bleak at times, she has witnessed phenomenal things take place within organizations that other consultants wrote off as impossible and she is highly optimistic about the future of OT.

SUMMARY

This chapter looks at OT from a differnet angle. It presents predictions about the course of the phenomenon from the points-of-view of the fourteen OT professionals in this study. In so doing, it looks at the impact and contributions of OT, the resistances to the movement, the applicability of OT and its potentials for the future.

Impact/Contributions of OT

Most of the participants agreed that the current impact and contributions of Organization Transformation are negligible. Others say that the movement is steadily growing and gaining more impact. At least one participant believes that the future impact and contributions of OT may be insignificant; and yet others believe that the future impact will be great.

Shandler was one of those who said that the overall current impact of Organization Transformation is negligible; however, Shandler seemed more hopeful in his outlook for a future with slow but steady growth. John Adams also believes that OT has not had a widespread impact on organizations; however, he talks about transformation having a significant impact on individuals. According to Adams, the primary impact of OT thus far has been to legitimize the thinking of individuals who are pioneering this new way of viewing organizations. Looking to the future, Adams predicted that Organization Transformation will become a part of the "mainstream way of life." Bartunek's response had to do with her belief in the difficulty and painfulness of the transformation process. Like Bartunek, Kueppers acknowledged the painfulness of organization transformations; however, he believes that organizations are becoming far more productive as a result.

Katharine Esty talked about how OT has "infiltrated" organizations in an indirect, covert manner. Harrison Owen, like Esty, discussed the indirect impact of Organization Transformation on language and how it is increasingly becoming more acceptable as more and more authors write about the subject. Simmons' view was that, although Organization Transformation has had a positive affect on some organizations, the future economic impact on organizations in the U.S. will be poor due to current leadership in industry and government.

Carew talks about OT being a cultural movement that some Organization Transformation people are attempting to lead. He believes that the OT movement is a reflection of what is happening in the world. OT, according to Grant Ingle, is increasingly having impact; myth, ritual, symbol, vision are powerful variables and have probably been discovered before. Ingle says that OT has a rebelliousness about it which perhaps flows from the rebelliousness of the 1960s. Bryant Rollins talks about the fundamental impact of women and people of color on the transformation of organizations. Stetson-Kessler, like others, alludes to OT being a painful process; however, her metaphor for OT was "a little seed that's just beginning to sprout."

Resistances to OT

Participants acknowledged that current and future resistances to OT come from individuals, groups, and organizations—but primarily from individuals. The most common theme found in the responses is fear—individual fear of the unknown, as Rollins noted in his response. Anderson stated that there is a natural death and regeneration involved in transformation. Although some people are suffering under their current systems, they prefer to continue suffering rather than face the death and rebirth of transformation. Likewise, Stetson-Kessler points to fear; however, she specifically points to fearfulness by those with power, namely white males, who are the primary deterents to Organization Transformation. Grant Ingle, like Stetson-Kessler, describes the primary barrier as coming from white males.

Kueppers talks about individual resistances coming from displaced individuals. Shandler's response to the question has to do with the ability of OT practitioners to "honor" and manage resistances. Shandler sees resistance as a natural part of people's basic mind-sets. Adams says that the identification with money and power is the primary cause for resistance to Organization Transformation; and Bartunek discusses how fads tend to undercut the power of a movement such as Organization Transformation. Esty says that resistances to Organization Transformation come from a rational linear mind-set that is primarily masculine, and that OT tends to be more feminine. Gordon says that resistance comes primarily from people who want something more concrete to "grasp."

Applicability of OT

Esty, Adams, and Bartunek believe that there are some types of industires that are more receptive to OT than others. Gordon, Anderson, Carew, Owen, Rollins, Simmons and Stetson-Kessler say that Organization Transformation is equally applicable to all kinds of organizations. Shandler believes all organizations could benefit by OT, but some are more receptive than others.

Potentials of OT

Some participants are very optimistic about the potential of Organization Transformation's impact on the current environment, and others are quite pessimistic. Jean Bartunek paints a not-so-pretty picture of the future. She believes that in some ways there are large numbers of transformations going on that aren't happening in the way OT people like to talk about them. On the other hand, Norma Jean Anderson is very optimistic about the potentials of OT in the current environment. She believes that OT has high potentials and that social, economic, and even political systems can be transformed.

Esty's outlook is gloomy for the immediate future, but hopeful in the long run. She believes that the economy is probably going to turn sour primarily due to our inability to handle the competition overseas. She believes that as companies go through their "lean and mean" stages, people will gradually become more open to Organization Transformation. Likewise, John Adams states: "In the short term I'm pessimistic, however, in the long term I'm very optimistic. I think maybe we need to go through a kind of a cleansing; a phoenix move to get to the other side."

5

The Case

The case provided a tangible vehicle for the participants to discuss their ideas, theories, and interventions in organizations. It was included to provide a more "standardized" piece to the data-analysis process. This chapter presents the case findings, which are summarized at the end.

Every participant was presented with and responded to the following case, which was read aloud to them verbatim by the researcher.

You have been called in to consult with a medium-size, mid-western, member-owned organization that produces custom-designed office furniture. This organization has been in operation since the early 1920s. What has made this company different is its dedication to the promotion of democratic management principles. Its primary decision-making body consists of a Board of Directors elected by its members. The Chair of the Board is selected by the members of the Board, who serve in this position on a rotating basis. For the past ten years, this organization's rate of growth has gradually decreased as more competitors have come into the market. Internally, over the past ten years, the organization has experienced severe conflicts among its members over its mission, products, services, and general direction. The members of this organization have split into several powerful factions whose in-fighting has affected the quality of the organization's products and services.

Each participant was provided with a copy of the case to read as the researcher read the case aloud. This procedure was designed to aid participants in answering the following questions:

- How would you intervene in this particular situation?
  Describe your intervention.
- What would you do differently from other consultants?
- What outcomes would you expect from your intervention?
  Describe those outcomes.

Unlike other chapters, this chapter presents excerpts from every participant's responses in epigrammatic form. These statements represent key ideas contained in the participant's answers to the three case questions. Great care was taken to use the words of participants, although the statements were edited for crispness and clarity. Also, responses to the case questions are presented in the order given by each participant and do not necessarily represent an order of priority or a step-by-step process.

HOW WOULD YOU INTERVENE?

The following are participant responses to the question: How would you intervene in this particular situation? Describe your intervention.

Adams

I'd want to know what the different factions were up to and see if there was any common ground possible.

I'd ask people first of all what their own personal vision is, and then ask them to describe what would help them, as much as an organization can help them, have their personal vision.

I'd ask, "What else would the organization need to really be excellent?"

I'd start putting together a common vision that everybody could identify with.

Some people would probably leave.

There could probably be a number of OD-type operations going on to work with the conflicts, to as much as possible resolve unnecessary intangible types of polarizations, to help people learn to know each other in more constructive ways, and so on—OD has a lot of technologies for doing that.

In order to not fall back into the same thing a year later, you can work instilling people with a sense of direction. The most critical intervention is making sure the board is together and has a clear sense of what it wants to be.

It has to have that top direction, some kind of compelling statement that the top management is willing to take a stand on. I think that would be a first critical thing.

And then, again, a lot of repair work, and communications work, and conflict work with various factions.

Making it clear that everybody doesn't have to like everybody—and everybody doesn't have to stay here. Some people can leave if they find they don't fit in with the direction we're moving in.

The top management term really has to make itself central.

Anderson

I'd talk to the Board concerning their role in the organization. What I'd want to know is how they view themselves; do they view themselves as policymakers or are they in the business of managing the organization? Sometimes boards get in the way of that.

I would have them clarify it with me, so that we could look at just how they see themselves.

I would work, also, with the manager of operations.

I would not only flesh out the role of the board, and their expectations of themselves, but also the board's expectations of the Manager, and the Manager's expectations of himself. I'd also have the Manager clarify his expectations of the board—how he feels the board should work with him or her.

And, I would get them together—the Manager and the Board—in terms of agreeing on these particular expectations.

It looks like this organization really needs transformation, because they have conflicts about what the mission is, and what kinds of products and services they are going to deliver. They don't come to any agreement in terms of general direction. So, therefore, it looks like it doesn't have enough pieces in order to warrant just being developed.

Most organizations at this stage are at a point called "organizational triage," where they may die. And I think I would bring this point out to them in terms of —this is a possibility if things aren't taken care of soon—let them know they're in dire trouble. They would make the decision as to whether they want transformation or whether they want death.

I would do an assessment of what has worked. And I would look at developing a method to accentuate the parts of their working habits that are not dysfunctional.

If they hadn't been doing anything together that's workable, then I would talk about creating a new organization. I mean, the same people could have a new orgnaization and start all over, from the ground floor—coming up with a mission, and goals, and objectives, and methods of working, and identification of services and clients, and what we are all about.

To create that new organization, I would work with the Board, in terms of their visualization of what they feel should be happening.

I would have the board send out a questionnaire to the membership.

I don't know what their organizational structure is, but if it is an identifiable structure, I would have particular groups of people meet together and talk about how they saw it. I'd get a perspective of the organization, not only from my perspective, but from the board's perspective, and from the members' perspectives.

I'd have them share this, with the object of them coming up with some kind of changes they all might go for. They'd visualize it and then they'd name it, and then, they'd begin to see what it takes to get there.

Bartunek

I would like to have some sense of how the in-fighting occurs—what are the natures of the conflicts.

I would like to have some sense of what the various interpretive schemes are—out of which people are operating, and why it is that the conflicts have occurred.

I'd like to know what the level of the disagreement is. Let me be more specific about that. Is this partly a difference in understanding of, for example, what "democratic management principles" mean? Or just what are the underlying issues?

That would be my first inclination, to try to get a sense of what the different interpretives are—what the real content of the conflict is, what the norms for conflict-handling are.

I think the way I would do that—I would have to be around for awhile. I couldn't just give them questionnaire tests, it would involve hanging out, it'd be interviewing people a lot, it would be sitting in on meetings and observing how conflicts are handled.

So, talking to people and different factions and finding out their perspective and who all shares it and who doesn't—that sort of thing.

I would be interested in the different factions, not only in their general sense of what the company should be doing, but their sense of how decisions should be made—the kind of structures they purpose to go with their underlying sense.

I think I would need to wait for a while before knowing exactly what to do. This is my general inclination as a way of approaching it, this is assuming that what's needed is a transformation of some kind, which I am not sure about at this point.

My general inclination would be to give some people in the company, first of all, skills at, appreciating a transformational perspective, and appreciating that if this is going to happen, it requires the different perspectives.

One kind of intervention technique that I think useful is what Mason and Mitroff call "strategic assumption surfacing." This is a milder version of what is also called the "dialectical inquiry method." They used it, for example, in consulting with some people in a census bureau where one of the problems was, how do you count people? Some people were saying you count everybody, and some people were saying, "But if you do that, you're going to find the unregistered—undocumented people, etc." Those were pretty fundamental disagreements. They found ways of using that process to help people surface the underlying assumptions behind why they disagree with each other, and eventually, over time, using dialectical processes—not just consensus type things—reach some sort of agreement on assumptions.

I would try to teach people dialectical inquiry skills and strategic assumption surfacing skills. The assumption is that the different perspectives could inform each other. Again, it would depend on my confidence that that's the issue.

The intervention would take a while.

Carew

First I would get more information. I'd really try to get a feel for what's going on in those different camps. I'd want to get some data about what has been the decline in order to really get a good sense of the framework of the organization.

I'd look at records, I'd talk to individuals in these various camps, I'd try to get a good sense of what the organizational mission, products, service, general direction, looked like from the perspective of these camps or factions. And then I'd share the data with the organization.

Depending on how large it is, the appropriate entry, whether it's just this Board of Directors, if the factions that are in the organization are also in the Board of Directors that are elected by the factions—if so, that probably would be a place to start, and to really work with that group around getting a clearer vision of what they want to look like. What would it be like ideally, not only in terms of what they're doing or producing, but what it's like to live in that organization. How they would like it to feel in that organization is part of the vision. That would be the first place, I think, that I'd start.

First get some sense of vision and goals; after that, begin to develop some strategies to get there. The first place they have to get on board is around some sense of mission or vision. Without having some alignment or some commonality around that, it's going to be almost impossible to get rid of those factions.

That's where I'd start—and how I'd carry it from there would really depend on what went on. I could probably use a much more Action Research approach to getting people involved and figuring out what needs to be done.

Standard, for me, would be first a diagnosis—finding out what the devil is going on; and then involving people in developing some action plans around moving from where they are to where they want to be is relatively simplistic, but it's not simple to carry out, so that would be fairly standard. What those action steps or strategies are would vary. Another standard approach would be insisting on somehow involving the people in the organization—not in every single thing, but in those strategies that they are going to be impacted by.

Esty

I would first try to develop a contract that allowed me to gather data about what's going on.

I would want to talk to people at every level. And I would want to do that by talking to individuals and also in focus groups.

In this case, I'd probably want to form some kind of a steering committee—advisory committee—say of twelve people in the organization to work with me. They would help me to figure out what questions I should ask—they'd help me to look at the data.

What I would do then is interview people, have focus groups; and I'd either do it alone or with a bunch of people, depending on the size of the organization and the size of their budget.

I'd gather the material and leave it somewhat in it's raw state, but do a little bit of analysis—enumerate what were the critical issues—then develop some sense of what I thought was going on with each critical issue. And then get them to look at it—using their own quotes and so on.

I'd also look at their documents and their personnel policies—some archival observations.

I'd also just look around—just observe—"what do I see?" I think you can learn a lot about organizations by going to the cafeteria.

I would work with the steering committee looking at this data. And then have them come up with some kind of an action plan—I would, hopefully, incorporate top management into the steering committee.

Then I would help with the implementation. I think one of the things that's different about my approach is that I really hang around for the implementation. The sense of what needs to happen is only the beginning, and I usually will try to contract in the very beginning for the implementation—so that afterward, when the steering committee comes up with an action plan, we would work together. And I would come back from time-to-time—once a month, once every six weeks—to work with groups that have been given the task of implementing the various pieces of the action plan.

So, this might take a year—this whole process. The assessment phase might take two months to three months—not long. I don't take long assessments. The real heart of the matter is the implementation of the changes. Sometimes I might do more work with the steering committee—continue to work with them after they've implemented a series of changes. Often, that group will implement another series of changes; it's kind of like cycles of changes.

Gordon

I'd have to establish that everybody's my client there—I'd have to have access to everybody there.

They would have to be open to letting go of certain opinions and beliefs about how to improve the company's performance and what the problems are. I would have to negotiate with my nominal client first of all to make that clear. My nominal client would be whoever is responsible for bringing me in, and who has ultimately the clout.

I would want to eventually cover everybody there. I would want to find out what their perceptions are. I'd want to meet first of all with the nominal client, and I would discuss their views. I would share what my approach would be, which is to have access to everybody within the organization, and to be able to work with everybody in the organization as well; and I'd get some early commitments about that.

I'd try to establish what they're committed to—the nominal client first. Then I'd also say, "I want to come back to you when I found out what other people are committed to as well." And so we have an ongoing, negotiate-renegotiate type of thing as we go along.

I'd make it clear that I'm not there to bring a solution—I believe the solution is already present, and so it really is about looking at how we cultivate that together.

I'd want to talk to people, on an individual basis; and there'd probably be times I'd want to talk to them as a group as well. A lot has to do with what happens during that first meeting. I wouldn't go in there with a fixed agenda, I would want to play it by ear and attend to what was happening as we went along, see how things were evolving.

My most important objectives in doing all of that would be establishing the relationship and the trust factor; I'm also modeling what I'm going to be doing right from the very beginning—that is, coming in without a lot of fixed opinions or views.

Ingle

First of all, I'd want to know about the gender and racial composition of this group; I might not be appropriate for the organization, maybe I shouldn't be there at all. That's the first concern.

The second concern has to do some sort of paid diagnostic, after which we would decide whether to take the client, and that's their opportunity to look at us too. The basic approach, which comes from OD—not so much from OT, is relevant.

That they're democratically managed I think is important; I would use a different style with them than I would with a sort of straight-line, private sector firm. I would insist that we probably perform some sort of joint diagnosis where I would insist on a mechanism or a process by which we would jointly conduct the diagnosis. They would be learning about how to diagnose their problems at the same time. So, in other words, we'd do the process and give them some clues about a process they could use in the future to find out what's going on—that grew out of my work with co-ops. I probably wouldn't do that with a more traditional organization because they wouldn't understand it.

Now first thing I'd ask them to do is to create a group, some sort of design team that represented all the different constituencies. That is part of, for me, a diagnostic phase. That's the group that helps us design the session in which we do joint diagnosis.

If their organization has a large proportion of women, and none end up on our design team, you say right away, "Whoa." So it gives you some very important clues. The other thing is that that group will probably serve as the major power brokers in the organization and contains one of the founders, typically.

My theory is that every interaction you have with representatives of the organization is like a hologram. If I'm meeting with you, and you're the client, imbedded in our interaction are all of the issues of your organization—this is true particularly in a group. So, you just have to be sharp enough to pick them out.

I'd attempt to use a model of sharing expertise and member education.

I'd want to use a style that was supportive of their particular form of democratic management. The single most critical act of my intervention would be to make sure that it supports instead of undermines the democratic process. I personally value that kind of organization—I think it's important. There are lots of ways of providing advice to them that would undermine them. Very manager-based interventions can create more power disparity.

This is the sort of the presenting problem: "There is severe conflict over mission, product, services and direction." Obviously, as you get into this, there's probably lots more behind that. But this suggests that you need some sort of intervention, which in OD you'd call team-building—but I would like something a little more radical, and some opportunity that's consistent with democratic culture.

My suspicion is also that the democratic culture has probably gone awry in this organization. I'd like to use the Harrison Owen model: creating an open space in this organization and letting people tell their stories. In his model, we'd be thinking about how to develop an integrated story for this organization; a story for the future.

Johnston

I would recommend to the top management that they consider an Organization Transformation approach which would start with something called "Open Systems Planning." What this could do is both heal the split that is occuring, and at the same time provide a vision of what this organization wants to become right now in light of the current market and all of the variables playing on the organization.

In terms of process, we would start with at least two days off-site with this top management group. And the first day we would take up the question, how does each organization that we do business with (whether outside the organization or inside) see us, and why do we think they see us that way?

Then, the second day we'd take up the question, how do we want them to see us, and why?

As focal points for those questions you might have ten or twelve different organizations or sub-organizations, including employee groups. How does this particular contingent of people see us? How does the engineering group—if there's an engineering organization—see us? So you take every major population or sub-population and focus on them as separate groups. Outside the organization, it could be the suppliers, it could be clients, it could be the market as a whole—segments of the market. Any particular significant group that impinges on or influences the success, or lack of success, of this organization.

Once you've done that, you take that data and set up interviews with representative samples of each of these organizations, and share that data with them and ask them if it's valid, and if it isn't, ask for the discrepancies? Or just go out and question them—interview them, and find out how they feel in response to the same questions.

And then come back, pool all that data, and analyze it, synthesize it, and look for common themes, dissimilar themes, and go from there in terms of creating with top management not only the vision, but also the process and the interventions for bringing that vision to pass.

Open Systems Planning is not new; however, I invented my own particular approach to applying it. I added some action steps to it. Also, the original concept didn't include a verification of the data; it just included the two-day or three-day off-site data gathering with the client group.

Kueppers

The primary way I'd intervene would be with the Board of Directors as to the mission of the organization—it has to get clear within the Board.

If the organization is really democratic, one of the things that needs to come out is that this Board of Directors have been given the power by the electorate, made up of members of the organization.

The Board has to come to grips with the mission of that organization, and there has to be a solid commitment behind that, so it'd be, as much as possible, a consensus as to what that mission statement is. That's what I would work on first and foremost, what are we about? Who are we? All the team building and organizational stuff I do starts from that premise.

From the mission comes the particular roles and responsibilities.

Once we define our mission, I would put that out to the populace. In fact, I've just been doing this work in organizations, so, this is pretty real to me. Take that out to the various constituencies and say, "This is what we're about, and how can we sign you up to that." That's the process you go through—you find out what they need to come on board, and what are the resistances. So, you have to "sell it down the line."

You also have to figure out how each person is going to fit in his or her role within that organization.

Owen

Well, at the point that you left it there I'd let 'em go and fight until they got pretty serious. I mean what's described there is a sort of standard life-cycle. The possibility of meaningfully intervening would only take place when they recognize the necessity of everybody letting go.

It's pretty simple; you sit down and say "Folks, there's no major problem in turning this around. There is a major problem in you living with it after it's turned around, and if you are prepared basically to live with the results, no problem."

I'd help them to understand a little bit about what the grief work process is. It's not a great deal, they will go through it, you don't have to do anything; all you have to do is create the space to let it happen and pick up the pieces and help them be conscious.

Just in terms of intervention, I do very little, and I try to do less rather than more. But where I do a lot is at the end, to sit down with whoever is interested and say, "Ok, let's reflect on what it was you went through so the next time you get yourself into something like this you don't have to come bother me."

The biggest problem in that situation is getting folks to understand that there is no magic bullet. They can't have their cake and eat it too. There's no way to manage transformation. When it's over it's over.

Rollins

If they are not a culturally diverse organization, there are certainly women working in the organization—white women at any case. I would attempt to find out who these people are and what their style is.

A preferred intervention would be to begin by working with the Board; and then as quickly as possible with key stakeholders in the system—whoever that might be.

I'd have to know more about the department heads, about the electoral process. Is it a general election, or is it through departments? Are the people representative of the various departments, so that there are some stakeholder populations in there?

I'd talk to the Board in more depth, and then talk to some other stakeholders in more depth.

I think the first step would be to try to figure out what's going on, what people's perceptions are. And so there would be what we would call a lattice exploration—or environmental scan.

The kind of stakeholders I want to be talking to are not always the recognized people, but some of the people who are heroes and heroines down there in the system, who have insights and perceptions and information that would be useful to have.

What I'd want to get, either through that kind of process or maybe through a focus group process, would be a scan of what's going on in the perceptions of the people down in the system. What's going on internally, and what's going on out there with the clients, and how it's affecting consumers—get a picture of what's happening.

Now, depending on the actual demographics, if it were feasible, and if it made sense in terms of how they see the issues—it might not, so we certainly would be careful about not working our issues—but if we get a sense that there were some issues that were race- and gender-oriented, we'd get some perceptions on what those race and gender issues are from the general organization by talking to some of those folks; we'd see them as another group of key stakeholders in the process. The way we do that is by dividing groups throughout the system—again lattice, by Black men, Black women, Hispanic men, Hispanic women, and so forth, and getting their individual perceptions of what's happening around race and gender, and what's happening in the company—systemically.

We would want to spend some time with the officers and the people who are basically running the company.

We do a structured process of diagnostics, and we would be asking all of these groups of people: What are the issues? What events contribute to their assessment? We'd ask for description of the issues regarding internal conflicts and consumer-market conflicts or inadequacies.

We would do some visioning with them, "Where would you see this organization going—the best of all possible worlds?" "Where would you want to be a year from now?" Just to get a sense of where they want to go—and what kind of steps that might be taken to help them to get there, from their perspective.

Then we would combine all of that in some way, and then present it back to the Board of Directors.

At that point, we normally suggest a three-day or four-day retreat that combines several things. Depending on what we find, it combines strategic planning, some team building and, if it were appropriate, some work on race and gender issues. We would offer the feedback initially in a Board meeting, but then say, if you really want to get into these issues we'd suggest you need to go off-site and spend three or four days doing some work.

So here's the first phase, which is essentially an environmental scan diagnosing whatever we can fairly quickly—as to what's going on, gathering the data together, making the initial presentation to whomever the client is, and then suggesting that we need to go into this in some depth—"Let's go off-site and really take a look at what's going on here, and do some work with it."

We would then work from there to design that kind of event. Depending on what they want to achieve, we would help them to decide who should be there. We would work with them—consult with them as to who should be there.

A lot depends on the style of the Chair of the Board. When we can, we go through a visioning process with that person, which is an individual two- or three-hour session where we go in-depth with the leader of the organization around what he or she is trying to achieve, what her or his values are, what her or his vision is, where her or his driving is. Now in a democratic arrangement it might be different, so there would be clealy some consulting relationship with the senior—with the person who is in the leadership position.

The way we work with strategic planning and team building is we make some assumption that the most effective organizations are driven by their values—that's the assumption we bring. That is one of the reasons that mission statements frequently wind up on company's walls, and don't mean anything. So, it's very important to go through a deep process with the Board, for example—or key people. To give them a chance to talk about why they are donig what they are doing, why is this important to them anyhow.

It begins with their values. I'll be more specific. The way we think about values is that our values are our best selves. When I was growing up in Roxbury, my parents told me how to live the best way I could—they imbued me with a lot of values around honesty and openness, and things like that. They said, "You live according to these values, and you're going to achieve your best self—you're going to have your best shot at getting what you want to achieve in your life." So these values represent your best self.

We have values that are personal, organizational, and professional. Sometimes they are all the same, sometimes they are very different. So we get the group of people thinking about their personal values and writing them down. And then we get them to talk about them, share them out. They can draw pictures, there are all kinds of ways that they can express what their values are. The important thing is to get them out in public.

And then we ask them, "What are all of the things that have been happening in this organization over the last six years, or whatever time period, that have supported your values?" and, "What are all of the things that have violated your values?" and then "What are all of the things that you've done in the last six years, given these values, that have been supportive of your achieving these values?" and "What are all of the things that you have done that have violated your values?"

So, we get into deep issues around people doing things, or being in situations in the organization where they've violated their own values. We heard people say, "Well, yeah, we made this decision around that, but we didn't tell our people the whole story because we didn't think they could handle it, and one of my most important values is honesty and integrity, and damn it, when we couldn't tell our people the truth, I didn't like it at all. Did we have the choice? Maybe and maybe not, but I didn't like it at all!"

Then it gets to: "What are our processes—what do we do that supports our values, and what do we do that violates our values? And it's a facilitative process. I'm talking about their interactions—how we make decisions, how we relate to each other, so forth. So we get into a fairly substantial process, and it takes some time. We get people talking about what's really important to them in their lives, in their families, in their professions, and in the business.

The purpose is not to come out with something that they can agree on—the values of this organization. Values are non-negotiable, so we are not trying to get a consensus on the values, not even the core values. Sometimes we ask them to talk about what their core values are, but our intent is not to consciously or overtly get them to compare values, but simply to accept that there are differences. Values are the hardest thing to negotiate, and are conceptually nonnegotiable.

The next step is vision. We get them into a visioning process, and that can go in a number of ways. So, "Given my values, this is my vision." Then there are some real differences, or there are some similarities, and some reaction and discussion around what the vision is, and then that's where we start to make comparisons and the process that we call "alignment."

It's very important for there to be alignment on the vision. It doesn't mean agreement, because there may be some things that people disagree on around vision, but at least there is some way of alignment then—"let's form an agreement." And the notion is that if you don't have a vision, or if you don't have a port in mind if you're the captain of a ship, then "any wind is a fair wind." So, in order to pick the wind that you want that's going to get you where you want to go, you have to know where you want to go—you have to have a vision.

We get the visions articulated. It may be the leader's vision, but the people say, "I buy into it, but you've gotta change this or I can't buy into that." It's a whole process.

In the values part we're working on the communications issue as well, so that if there are some conflicts in communicating that violate people's values, we begin to create some norms, and ask them, "What norms do you want to live by in this room to get through the next step of this process, given your values?" So we begin to work with them around how they are going to function as a group.

This is a process that evolves over time, and basically says that this group of people can solve their own problems—they can address the internal conflicts, they can get a better share of the marketplace, if the relationships are solid, if they're talking straight to each other, if they're energized and going after it, if they're in alignment as to where they are trying to go, and if they do that for the total organization—down the system.

Everything they need is right there—it's in the room, and it's in their organization. And then the question is, "What tools do we need to get it out into the total 13,000 people?" And then you start to talk about processes for moving it down into the system.

Shandler

The very first thing that I'd do is interview all of the Board members, and a selection of individuals at lower levels of the organization. I'd spend several days, probably, interviewing people and finding out what's really going on as seen by the individuals in the organization.

The interviews would be anonymous, but not confidential. Anonymous in the sense that I'd like to be able to use the information that the individuals give me, but not say, "Well, Beverly said—"; just say, "A perception in the organization is that—".

So once I have this information, I would do a number of things. The way you have this described here sounds like there is not only conflict and uncertainty at the top about the direction that the company is going in, but also a lot of stuff going on at the bottom. In this case, I would have to get the top team together, probably for three days, set them down and take them through, basically, hammering out the direction that they want to go in, and reaching consensus about it, as opposed to democracy.

I do not work on a democratic basis when I'm working with teams. I always work for a consensus.

We'd go off-site for three days, and basically hammer out, What is the vision of this company? What do you want to do? Where are you going? What do you want the value of this place to be?

There is a lot of stuff going on that is basically unhealthy, and I'd get them to articulate that.

I'd help them to establish a set of strategic-level goals. What are the basic strategic-level goals that need to show up that we can measure, so that we know that we're on track toward this vision?

So it is establish the vision first; then the goals, then responsibilities for each of the team members: who's going to do what, who's going to be responsible for what, who's going to be the champion for each of these goals. By the way, it just so happens that this particular case fits exactly the primary thing that I do. Then I would work backwards to the present.

I would basically unfurl the headlines that I gleaned from all of my interviews with them, which would deal with the conflict that existed on the team—in other words, all of the unfinished interpersonal business. What I would do is teach them a way to work through what I call grievances to the next level, which is a request for change. Implicit in any grievance that I might have with another person is a request for a change. I would help you to articulate the change that you want from this other person; then they would negotiate an agreement about that change. And then follow up and see if it works, and if it doesn't, go to the beginning again. Work it through until you have what you need.

I give them a process, and also might, if they request it, actually do third-party negotiations with them. But the end result that I'd be looking for is that there'd be no more what I call "caca" in the system. The system would be flushed, they would've been given an enema, the interpersonal stuff healed, and people could get on without putting their energy into their gunny sacks.

I would take a look at all sorts of win-lose dynamics that might be showing up. For example, structures—departments that are in competition with each other, perhaps that might show up as the result of interviews.

We'd also establish a sense of what are the ground rules, what are we going to play the game by. It sounds like this group does not have a clear code, a spoken code of conduct, and they don't know how to get through stuff. So, I would focus on a strategic direction, how we're going to live together, and healing stuff from the past.

Once that was done, I would help them—and this could be a fairly big project—translate the decisions that they made at the top into what I would call an enrollment process. In this case, I'd probably go department by department.

It sounds like intra-departmentally they have—it says here lots of personal conflict—that stuff would also have to be worked out. They'd be either taught a method for doing it, or in the form of some kind of group it could be done, or it could be done in third-party negotiations. And then also at a departmental level, and inter-departmentally, I would get them to focus on, how can we basically achieve the grand design—the grand vision as proposed by the Board? Since it's elected by them—how can we do that? And I would really work hard toward creating a critical mass of people moving in the same direction.

They would have to take a look at the business level. Why are the competitors basically beating the pants off them? They'd have to take a look at design issues, which may mean that the competitors are getting raw materials cheaper, or they're having it made off-shore. What are the reasons that the competition is beating them? They'd have to take a very honest look at that. They may have to get off some of their ways of doing things.

Are they overstaffed? They might have to take a look at some very hard things that nobody feels comfortable about. Do they need to introduce new products? Maybe they can use their technology and their expertise for developing new products. Maybe they haven't kept up with what's happening in the marketplace. Maybe they have all sorts of opportunities.

Anyway, that's sort of the jist of what I would do with it. It would be very definitely an organizational-wide intervention, and it would be a top-down intervention. It would have to start from the top, because if they weren't walking their talk—if I didn't have them behind me, I'd never touch this one with a ten-foot pole.

Simmons

The first thing that I would do is to sit down with the Board and ask them why they think they need a consultant, and spend a good deal of time pushing on that question.

The second thing that I'd do is to do an organizational diagnosis with a consulting team.

This entails interviewing Board members individually and then a diagonal slice across the organization. Probably focus groups at the plant level. I'd feed that back to them, and make recommendations as to things that I think they can work on, and things that they need some help working on.

I think that the next step would be to work in those areas. And clearly, one of the things that they need is consensus around a mission statement.

They may be weak on consensual decision making; a lot of worker-owned firms are. Therefore, I would be sure that they have the tools to work effectively in that way.

I'd probably also do some team building around the tasks—around some of the easier tasks that they can work on without outside help.

Phase I would be assuring that they have some skills around the deficits they have, and then including the team building and consensus decision making, and then moving them into developing a real mission statement.

Now, there may be some information deficits, so they're some real problems deciding what to do and this has caused some of the conflicts. It may be important for them to clarify their vision of what the organization is all about. And, if they haven't done that, then as part of the mission development stage, they should go through some visioning.

As preparation for the visioning, it may make sense to have them go out and see some other firms that are in the same business. And if it means going abroad, if they have an unlimited budget, then I would take them to Japan and Sweden and plan an awareness-creation experience for them—so they would see, sort of, next-generation products, and also understand some different styles—of how democratically managed organizations can operate. They should probably also visit other firms in this country. I think that would be the beginning.

I think the contracting and diagnosis is probably the most critical part of the intervention because that's where most of the mistakes are made; expectations aren't clear to the client, or the consultant doesn't understand what the real issues are.

Stetson-Kessler

I think the first thing that I would do would be to collect as much information as I could from the people who are on this Board. I would want to sit and talk with all of them at great length around who they are, what they think the primary focus of the corporation is, where it's headed, why it's headed in that direction, and what it is that they would like to see different. And just find out what's going on.

I would talk with individuals. When there's discord, my experience has been that it's usually a case of miscommunication. And goes back to my basic belief that we're all connected, and we're all one in some fashion. So, if we're not taking care of each other, if we're not cohesive, that it's just a misunderstanding of some sort—a dis-ease. So, I'd want to talk to everyone, only because that's the only way I would have of really feeling comfortable. I trust my analytical skills in that regard.

The next step in my style would be to get them all together and just feed them back what I heard in a way that would be non-threatening and non-exposing: "There's information here that maybe ought to be put out in the air." My experience with that is that it's a very freeing activity, and that people then begin to deal with the real issue because now it's out—it's not a secret that's being hidden anymore. The ability of people to deal with themselves once they have the data out is unlimited, from my experience.

I would ask every single person that I talk with, what would be the best way to feed them back what I have heard—so that it wouldn't be a threatening feedback. It would be what they all told me they wanted—and how they wanted to hear it—that's my preferred style, and it's never failed yet, in my experience.

I would want to know what the Board would want, what might be a next step. It could be to do some similar sorts of things with individual work groups, or however this company functions. It sounds like there might be a lot of artistic furniture engineers, or whatever. So there would probably be a need to pay particular attention to some of the functional things that go on. And then have some kind of sharing across the lines of the organization.

I think I would also want to look—just because of my own personal value system—at the demographics of the organization, and find out who's got the power and who doesn't, and what kind of people are employed here—what do they look like. And make some observations back to them. Lots of times what we see in organizations is that things are really out of balance. The worker level is all female, or all people of color, and if there's nobody in the hierarchy that represents that constituency, then there's going to be a problem.

Sometimes all it takes is just pointing out, "If this organization were to look in the mirror, this is the way it would see itself—how do you feel about that?" Lots of times people are horrified when they have themselves presented to themselves that way—it violates their value system. And the first thing that people in organizations say to us is, "But I'm a Christian," and we say to them, "Well, what does that mean to you?" "Well, I believe in people—that all people are equal." "Well, what does that mean to you?"—we just keep asking them. And they usually just talk themselves right into "God, I've got to do something about this—this is terrible."

So, I would ask a lot of questions and voice what I see in a nonjudgemental way, just to describe what it looks like to me as if I just landed here from Mars—"This is what I see." That is an intervention technique that is invaluable.

WHAT WOULD YOU DO DIFFERENTLY?

Participants were asked the question: "What would you do differently from other consultants?" They responded as follows:

Adams

I would think that a traditional OD intervention would be to resolve the disagreements first and then try to bring harmony. I wouldn't look at disagreements first.

I would get the top team to be clearly together and excited about where are we going to get to in ten years.

And then asking the different factions as we start working with implementing the vision, the higher purpose, the "Why, in order to" kinds of questions to see where they can find common ground.

And doing the team-building kinds of things that would be necessary or the intergroup kinds of things that would be needed to create some new glue or some new connections.

Anderson

I think others may see the current organization as the only possibility. "This is what it is and what it has to be—let's look at, maybe, the product mix; or, maybe we'll change some of the services." Then they'd probably take a little piece of it and work on it. I'd go for the big picture, "Maybe we're doing it all wrong." I think an Organizational Development person would also look at the way people work together—they look at team building. I think that they'd build a team for the same mission and the same goals; it would still be a piece of it, but a human piece of it as opposed to the functional piece of it.

Carew

Some people might go in and just work on conflict resolution right from the beginning without visioning, and mission development, and goal setting—I don't think that makes a whole lot of sense, given this little scenario.

Somebody might be more into the financial, in terms of marketing, they might focus on a narrower aspect as their intervention. Some might focus on management development—training in conflict management or something. So, there are a lot of different things that might be appropriate, but I would start with the vision.

Esty

I think that we're more collaborative. I don't think that everybody has this advisory committee. I think not everybody uses focus groups—I do a lot more group interviews.

I think it's more interesting, and it's also more of an intervention—it can reach a lot more people quickly.

The sense of implementation is different, and I think I also come from a theory that's different from most people's, which is this whole idea that we look at the organizational variables—look at the systems. I think that most people are trying to fix something—they look at trying to change the people. So, for instance, in my intervention I'd be looking at the recognition-and-reward system, the decision-making system, the hiring system, the career development system—and that's what I'd focus on, not the leadership, or individual people.

Gordon

Others may focus on the structure—seeing what the layouts are, seeing what the paperwork is. I don't want to see any of the paperwork for one; don't show me anything about the history or the profits or the losses. I don't need to see any of that on going in.

I don't necessarily need to know anything other than who's inviting me in, and perhaps those who are making decisions. I don't need to know the organizational structure, the hierarchy—that's not all that important. Whereas others may have those things foremost in their minds; that is, organizational structure, job classifications, duty statements, what kind of work people are doing and what they're getting paid for—structural type things. I think that out of my approach would come the appropriate structure, but I wouldn't go in there looking at the structure, or necessarily what people feel that I should be looking at.

I wouldn't even worry about the conflict piece yet, because again, that's symptomatic; I'll be trying to look at the cause. I wouldn't put those people together in, let's say, third-party conflict resolution. That would be crazy—that would be premature without understanding what's going on. I would have to have a sense of the larger view—does anybody have a vision?—and if it's shared.

Ingle

I'm not going to go in there and just do team building and strategic planning. I feel that those are tools, instrumental tools that can be applied inappropriately.

I have major questions about what the myth, rituals, symbols and so forth are and I will bet, from my own experience with this type of organization, there is a major split between democratic principles upon which the firm is founded and its day-to-day operating stuff. That's the history of the evolution of these organizations. I've worked with firms like this that are going private; they're getting rid of worker ownership—being fed up with it.

So it's really important to find out—get some sense of where they want to go. There's a tendency on the part of consultants a lot of times to say "Well, I'm the consultant, I know what way it's got to go." That can be very inappropriate, particularly with this organization. What they may need to do is end up creating some rituals of democratic self-renewal.

I'd also be worried about founders. Founders have often terrorized democratic organizations. We're all equal here, but—founder's disease is very common.

Vision: the common kind of thing to do is to get folks to agree on what the critical aspects or dimensions of the future are, and you can plug them into that vision—myth and values, membership, ten or fifteen things. Agreement goes a long way in a democratic organization. So maybe working with the Board—get them to agree on these dimensions as a very powerful first act of agreement. There are lots of ways to build a united vision.

There may be a split in the organization and the organization has got to decide; it may have to split into two groups; it may have to say goodbye to some folks—people may have to leave. It may have to be changed. It may be to the point where compromise can't happen.

I find that in most organizations if you ask people what their vision of the future of the organization is, they're grossly disparate, they haven't talked about it before, but they're all acting as if their particular vision is true. And a lot of the fighting is that somebody wants a lot of growth, somebody else thinks small is beautiful, and they're both acting as if that were true. So behind the scenes every time this person wants to do an expansion, this person is giving him or her hell—and because they sense conflict they avoid talking about this. So consultants are hired to say the unsayable and do the undoable.

Johnston

I think, basically, the difference is that I'm taking into account variables that can be seen as more holistic than those considered by the typical OD person I have known over the years.

I assume we are all one whereas I believe most OD people assume we are each separate from one another and the cosmos.

I believe the approach that I have is more proactive than the typical reactive approach of the usual OD person.

I assume a Jungian-like model of the human being, which consists of thinking, feeling-emoting, sensing, and intuiting—the spiritual; and when I do survey-feedback kinds of things, I take into account all of those basic elements as well as interpersonal.

I'm taking into account the transpersonal, the individual, and the interpersonal, not only in my diagnosis of the organization, but also in the design of the interventions.

The single most important element of my intervention is starting off with the question, who are you in the universe? Not only in terms of the universe of the marketplace, but, who are you? Then the questions, what do you want to be? What do you want to become?

What that does is give me, as well as the client, if the answers are pursued far enough, a sense of—a spiritual foundation, and also a sense of ultimate purpose that transcends the temporal level of life.

Transcend means to rise above the temporal everyday life of the organization. It goes beyond that, and then comes back to say, "Well, here's what we are, in light of the ageless—in light of the infinite—as constituents of it." I believe that that kind of awareness and consciousness breeds, not only in me as I've seen it in my own life, but breeds in the client a better perspective and sense of balance. Such clients are far less likely to be sexists, racists, and agists, or go out and rape and pillage the environment by dumping chemicals into the local streams and rivers.

Kueppers

I think most consultants worth their salt would probably work on mission.

Most of the people that I associate with are on the same wave length as I am, so I can't say how much differently.

One of the things that I do as a consultant is try to establish levels of trust—higher levels. One of the main ways I'd do that is to really honor where a person is at a particular time, and really encourage, and I become vulnerable myself. Part of how I do that is by taking some risks in the organization. And I also encourage the Chief Operating Officer, or the President, or the highest-level manager that I'm working with, to be vulnerable—willingly take a risk and put our guts on the line.

Also honoring what's going on at that particular time. I'd say to you—say if you're my CEO—"I recognize what's going on here is that you're playing games with Margaret over here." Or, "You're playing games with Robert—well, you're not being straight with him at all—you're saying that you want a team here, and you're going around this guy—cut the shit, what do you want to do?" So I point out their behavior to them.

My guiding operating principle is that I treat every conversation I have with my client as though it might be the last. That is, I put things out because they need to be put out there, not because I want to come back and be on the company payroll for the duration of a project.

That's me as a consultant being authentic; that's honoring my stuff to help them honor their stuff, so they can honor the people they're dealing with—it's all connected, there is just no division line here. I have to come to grips and put my job on the line; and the fact is, that's how it feels, putting my job on the line—my contract with my client on the line.

What actually happens is that it's so real, and they want to hear reality. They don't like it, they resist it, but they want to hear it, all the same. And they might want to shoot the messenger, and generally they don't shoot the messenger; but if they do, they know that they are shooting the person who had the truth—and they respect that fact. Usually, they just resist the messenger initially; and they sometimes shoot you—I've been shot down. The thing is your ego stays more in place when you are authentic than when you play games; your ego gets out of place when you camouflage.

So, putting myself on the line, to answer your question, What do I do differently? Hopefully, I bring in a higher level of authenticity, and honesty, and challenge, to my client. I would hope that any OD consultant does that. But certainly the consciousness of it that I bring in helps me to actually do that.

It's coming in with that level of caring for myself and caring for the client; caring for myself to honor what's going on here; caring for the client that I will give you the straight scoop; and knowing that it will be what is also needed for the organization.

There is some short-term pain. So, what do I do that's different? I don't know how much that's real different, but it certainly is done out of a perspective that everybody wins in that. And that's part of what makes it easier to do, and makes it easier to have it come out more crisply and consciously—I'm always very conscious of what I'm doing.

Owen

I don't know about what most other folks do, but I think there are some people who still seriously think that you can manage your way into a transformed organization, and I've got to say I don't think you really can. They're certainly not talking about the world that I'm living in; it's only useful for certain prescribed circumstances.

For me, when I start working with a client and they want to know what's going to happen, I have to say "I haven't the faintest idea. I can tell you some things that are likely to occur, not in detail. I can tell you some things that have occurred in other places. I could almost guarantee you that if they were to happen here it would be wrong. We've really got to find out where you are, what's happening, and get on with our business, and there are absolutely no guarantees."

Rollins

At some point along the way, we always work race and gender issues. They are not interested in that in this case, unless you overlay it, but at some point it's got to be an issue. So, that's one thing that we always bring out.

We don't work from a theoretical base, we follow the tide—we follow the group. So we don't bring in the kind of B-School orientation, we don't do a lot of statistical diagnostics—we do action research.

There are a lot of people who do action research. I think that the greatest distinction is that when we bring a team in, no matter what it's for, it's *always* diverse. We are always working diversity issues at a conceptual level, always looking for it—looking for opportunities—and not in an active way. Sort of in a passive, "wait a minute" way; and we are the models for how you could be in this area, and it *always* comes to the surface. And we find that those are the most liberating issues, when we get to work those. Because of who we are, it's almost always the case.

In the kind of three-to-five day strategic planning that I just described, race and gender issues come into focus. Frequently, those are the issues that break the group open and get people to talking.

Shandler

I imagine that an OD person would certainly do a lot of interviewing, and would concentrate on the interpersonal stuff—they'd pick right up on that, and might even help them with strategic planning—I don't know.

I guess this is the big difference: I would teach these people the answer to the basic question of who's responsible for the success of this organization. And the correct answer to that, even if it's not true, is that I am. I as an individual am 100 percent responsible. I would get that across, and I would get them to commit to it.

I would get people to put on these glasses and to look at this situation from the point of view of, I as an individual am 100 percent responsible for the results that are showing up, namely, that this organization is doing badly, and is riddled with conflict and doubt. Now, in the sense I am 100 percent responsible, even if it's not true, what am I going to do proactively to change that? Now, if I'm the Chairman of the Board, there are a lot of things that I can do, because I've got lots of power up there. If I'm on the Board, there are also lots of things that I can do. But if I'm a middle manager in this group, there are also lots of things that I can do—one thing that I can stop doing is saying, "Well, I don't have any power in this situation." If I'm a worker in this situation I can say, "You know, I'm an owner here, and I'm not happy with the results that are showing up." For example, "I'm going to make suggestions about new products that can be developed." Or, "A new way of doing things that will save a half an hour of time, which will save us twenty dollars in our production process."

Finger-pointing doesn't help. So, we're basically getting them to take responsibility themselves for the future. "OK, here's the situation, some poor results have been showing up, how can I move this organization forward?" Coming up with answers. I would absolutely inculcate that. And that's where the personal transformation notion does come in. I think that's the biggest difference between what I would do as an OT person, and what I might have done as an OD person.

Simmons

I don't know. I've done a lot of work in democratically managed firms, in fact I'm the Chairman of the Board of a democratically owned firm, a construction company. So, I have some understanding about the dynamics of these operations. And, second, I'm not trained as a professional OD person.

I came into this from an economics background. So, I don't know a lot of these distinctions, but I guess that one possible area is that I would really deal with the power issues—that's very important up front.

I would also really try to get them to develop their vision; and I'm not sure how important that is to the average OD practitioner—I know it's now a common sort of technique, but I don't know how common it is.

Stetson-Kessler

I always work with a partner, and it's much easier to do the work because there is always somebody watching from the other direction. We always work in differentiated race and gender teams. We feel much more confident about covering the whole field. I only have my own orientation, I get so stuck in it that I can't see other ways.

I do not know of any other firm that does that. And we get questioned an awful lot by clients, but our success rate is almost infallible. We will tell people right up front, "This is the way we work." And they'll say, "Well, that's really strange." And the curiosity factor will sometimes be why they want to work with us. Our experience is that there is something deep within them that makes contact with what it is that we're all about; and we trust that. We certainly don't talk about it with them until after we get to know them because they'd probably say "Get out of here!"

WHAT OUTCOMES WOULD YOU EXPECT?

Finally, the participants were asked, "What outcomes would you expect? Describe those outcomes." The responses were:

Adams

Excitement; positive energy rather than combative and negative energy; a sense of purpose; being more flexible. I would see people at more levels having a forum for bringing out their ideas and having them heard. I'd see a lot of internal, self-correcting mechanisms that would help people stay in touch with each other and promote communications and renegotiations wherever necessary. Healthy profits; healthy return on investments; probably a lot of leadership from a lot of different quarters—everybody basically is a leader; people taking a lot of initiatives, not asking for permission;

commitment to each other; increased awareness of an energy going into the organization as a member of the larger community that it's in; having more of flow in and out of the community.

Anderson

I'd walk into this organization and everything's vibrant! People are busy—people are touching one another, through their words and through their work, and through their beings. They know what they are about, they know what their mission is, they are working toward it. They are putting out a successful product. They are serving the people—there are no complaints about what is happening there. They are in touch with and communicate with the Board of Directors. The members of the Board of Directors are proud to be on the Board of such an organization. The Board's working well together. The Chair of the Board and the Manager of the organization are communicating frequently. They are in tune and aligned with the same goals. There is no in-fighting. People are talking about them. They are written about as being a new shining star serving the world. People apply from universities to the HRD person who comes to recruit. Students are in line trying to be interviewed for any openings that may come to them. They now see themselves empowered, each employee. There is no competition between them, but more competition within themselves in terms of doing a better job, day to day.

Bartunek

The general thing it would look like if I were successful would be some basic shared sense that where we're going is OK—even though not everybody would agree. There would be more skill in dealing with conflictual issues, and more of a sense of ways of surfacing them and letting them come out into the open. Also, if I were really successful, the people in the organization would have an understanding of what was happening. There would also be an increased sense on their part that people have perspectives out of which they operate, and that those perspectives have costs and benefits. So in one sense it is like they *have* the perspectives rather than *are* the perspectives—so they have some appreciation of what they are operating out of, rather than just sort of operate out of it and then getting mad at other people.

Carew

I would expect that we might have some struggles, but I would expect that we would come up with a vision to which people are committed—and some excitement about it, and in that process a resolution of the factions. Because if we can get to a clear sense of where we want to go together, most of the other things, I think, can be worked out. Without that clear sense, it's really tough to work on problems.

Esty

I'd expect a lot of change. Measurable results I think that we often look at are turnover and, also, our efforts in diversity: how many, what rank they get to. Sometimes it's sheer numbers of who's where. Again, sometimes we get numbers when we do assessments, we often do pre- and post-assessments. The other things, I think can't be measured, so, I would go back and try to ask about those things—things like job satisfaction, satisfaction with these various systems, and so on. I would expect the outcomes would be that systems would be different; the conflict-resolution systems, the recognition systems—I would expect some systems having been adjusted or changed dramatically. Then, I would expect that people would be happier—more committed.

Gordon

I think that there would be a clear sense of direction that not only focuses on what it is that people are needing to do now, and next year, and the year after, but a longer-range vision—and it would relate to the benefit of all concerned. That means the individuals in the company, the clients that they're serving, whatever they're in business to do, it would embrace and encompass all. There would be a sense of clarity about that, and a commitment to taking the steps necessary to achieve that.

Ingle

That I've supported the basic values and premises of the organization. That if it's a democratic organization, and wants to continue as such, that somehow I've strengthened that, or at least strengthened those processes that they hold dear, or buttressed what they say is important—that's number one. Number two, that in interacting with them—I don't like mystifying skills, so we've done something around strategic planning. It's like when you're giving someone a fish versus teaching them to fish. They somehow are left with a knowledge of how to do what we've helped them to do.

Johnston

Basic changes in assumptions about who and what they are, and their beliefs, their values, their attitudes, and their behaviors—this constitutes a major shift in all of those dimensions. For example, if this organization had seen itself as strictly a "moneymaking machine" before, with the kinds of questions I ask, and then the resulting vision that ensues from that group. They shift in a sense of themselves to, not just a moneymaking machine, but really a vital constituent of, not only the earth, but also the universe. And that they have a responsibility and accountability—not only to themselves, but also to everybody else in human society. That, to me, constitutes a transformation. It starts with self-image, a sense of self-worth, identity. It transcends individual ego, not only of the executives in charge, but also the organization.

Kueppers

A much greater sense of who an organization is as a working entity; a greater sense of freedom, of relaxedness, therefore, greater productivity; greater willingness to put ideas forth and have them be honored; a more fully functioning unit; the Board members would have a far greater sense of respect for one another that would filter down. We might make the decision, by the way, that we need to close ourselves up—or sell out. That might be a hard one, but as long as everybody's in tune with it, that is the reality. Let's say they found a particular direction to take the company, they'll have far more concerted efforts and energy pulling in the same direction, or moving in the same direction. You talk here about a lot of different factions—a lot of bickering. Well, a lot of the bickering comes about because it's squashed down energy that's coming out in some way. It's not honored energy—it's frustrated energy. And what this does is allow all that stuff to come and start to pull in the same direction. Or, for those who can't pull in that direction—we have to define who we are, and if you can't go in that direction, there is, perhaps, another organization out there that might be more aligned with who you are; I'm not saying that there aren't any variations on the theme, again. But that's what I would expect as an outcome, and I've seen it work.

Owen

That's very easy. I don't know what you'd see, but what you'd experience is just an incredible sense of joy. It's the kind of thing like with the group at Owens Corning. They walked out of there saying, "This is the most meaningful thing that's ever happened." And this was not an off-site, this was not the weekend on the mountaintop; this is working a real live business problem. I mean they were like the Redskins after the Super Bowl in the locker room. I mean, literally, these are staid old midwesterners. They're pouring champagne over each other's heads. Midway through this thing, they decided to give it a name—they called it the "Mash" team, Make Amazing Shit Happen. This is a Fortune 500 whatever—it's just exciting. We did a working model in eight days with $35,000; where conventional wisdom was talking it would take a year and a million and a half. So you can measure it that way. But that to me is not the significant measure. The significant measurement really is some kind of a quantum of joy release, because that's what's gonna give 'em the oomph to do it again.

Rollins

You'd find people talking openly to each other. You'd see people looking for feedback. You'd see a very high level of awareness and skill in talking about the effect of racism and sexism on work groups and committees and task forces—that would be just a part of the culture. You'd see an open system. You'd hear people who have a clear sense of what the vision is—and have, to some degree or another, bought into it—who understand why they are doing what they are doing, and how it contributes to the whole. You'd see relatively little bureaucracy and hierarchy. You'd see people talking to the President and the Chairman of the Board, and it's also "Joe" or "Jane." I think what you'd experience primarily is—somehow there is a spiritual aspect of it, and I don't mean that in a religious sense, but somehow there is something that people are sending out that goes beyond what they seem to be doing and have created. It seems to transcend the products that they're producing, it seems to transcend the individual relationships, there is something here that's bigger than what we can comprehend—they feel it, and know it. As an outsider, I know that something's going on there. It's not easy all the time being there, because there are real conflicts that come to the surface and get worked a lot of the time—so it's not always comfortable or easy, but still it's a place that you want to be—it's a place where you feel that you can grow, and get support. A place where you can have objectives and goals and a vision of your own and have them met to a greater degree. Where the organization's vision is sometimes subsumed on occasion, to an individual's vision. And then you'd see a real firm relationship with the outside world. In fact, you'd feel that there's not much of a difference between the inside and the outside—that the relationships that the company has with the consumer are as powerful as the relationships that the company has on the inside. They'd be spending a lot of time talking with consumers—they'd really have a feel for who's out there and what they want. They are in tune—they are tracking; they are appreciated—they are respected. You'd see a tremendous following of products. But I think most significant is what you'd feel, "There's something different going on here that's different from most organizations, and it's spiritual—a richness here."

Shandler

This could take a long time, Beverly, even if it was a relatively small organization. And one can be srong in determining a strategy. Let's say the price of steel went up a zillion percent, and they were absolutely depending on steel, it could put them out of business. Those things are realities that happen, and they happen all of the time. But assuming that the environment basically cooperated with them, they got their internal act together. It's not that they would not be fighting; fighting always happens when people chafe up against each other. But the individuals involved would not be fighting about "where are we going." They might fight about how "we're going to get there," or the best way to get there—I consider that to be healthy fighting. They would also not be gunny-sacking their grievances with each other; in other words, storing stuff up. The operating mode internally in the company would be win-win. "We're all in this together, and we're all going to do everything in our power to help the other person or the other department. We're all working for the sake of the accomplishment of the whole." Those are the major things. They might have the same equipment, or they might have different equipment, but it would be their basic attitudes and the way that they went about things that would be quite different.

Simmons

Unity of purpose; clear goals, roles and responsibilities; a vision that everyone shares; energy and creativity that you can't contain; and at the level of skills inside the organization, they could then fix their own problems in the future.

Stetson-Kessler

Presuming that this organization wants to have a growth rate that increases instead of decreases, that would certainly be an issue. If "in-fighting" is a negative sort of thing, my sense is that it would be—to the extent that they would want to have cohesion instead of conflict, those kinds of outcomes. That would be my direction with them; it would be their work, not mine. I wouldn't impose my own values on it. It would be my guess that whatever is going on in this group that makes the decisions, that once they've dealt with each other on a personal level, things would be different. They'd probably transform themselves rapidly into whatever it is that they want. I don't ever enter an organization with a presupposed notion of what they want. I know what I would want if I were there, and lots of times that's the stimulus I use to get them thinking about themselves, but not necessarily in any direction. I just use it as a tool sometimes saying, "How do we move so that we're getting at what you want?" And lots of times, when they can't articulate it, I'd say then "Well, if I were here—" and just sort of imagine it with them, "this is what I would do—" And they either immediately say, "Well, that's crazy." Or they say, "Yeah, yeah, that's what we want." And then that snowballs.

SUMMARY

The case provided a rich source of information about what Organization Transformation practitioners actually do. Some of the methods, techniques, procedures, and processes used by the participants appear quite common, while others were quite unique and even contradictory.

Starting with those common "elements," most of the participants thought it useful or critical to develop a "vision" for the hypothetical organization. Some of the respondents used the word "mission," while others used the word "vision." When the participants were queried about their definitions for the words, their answers were very much the same. The common elements in the different definitions for "mission" and "vision" may be summarized as: some future idea, concept or ideal for the organization that views the future state of the organization very differently from what can be seen in the structures and processes of the present. Perhaps the most critical commonality among the participants was their attention to "vision" and their focus on the organization as a whole.

Also common to the participants was their "point of entry" into the organization. Most of the participants commenced their interventions at the level of the Board of Directors, although they varied in the degree to which they accessed the rest of the organization.

Another common element among the interventions was a mixture of what appeared to be Organization Development techniques and the new OT concepts. For example, most of the participants had contracting, diagnostic and feedback phases to their interventions that parallel Action Research processes common in OD interventions. Also, many participants paid close attention to interpersonal interactions among members of the hypothetical organization, which included such things as team building and conflict resolution; these, too, are common OD technologies.

Another less tangible commonality among the participants' interventions was their recognition of something that transcended explanation, differentially called "energy," "joy," "commitment," and "spirit."

The differences were many, and involved varying techniques and approaches. The interventions ranged from those that appeared to be very much like OD interventions, such as the one described by Simmons, to those that were totally unique, like Owen's "open space" technology.

6

Summary and Conclusions

Revisiting the literature once again, John Adams (1984) states in his book, *Transforming Work*, that Organization Transformation is not a clear-cut discipline. There appears to be no universally accepted theory of OT among OT theorists and practitioners, even though there seem to be many commonalities in the way that OT is defined. On the surface, this investigation supports what Adams wrote in 1984. The fourteen participants in this study use a wide variety of methods and techniques, which are supported by an equally wide variety of theories and underlying concepts. And, as Adams described, there are also many commonalities in the way they define Organization Transformation, e.g., radical and fundamental change. When looked at it in a different way, it may also be said that OT encompasses a mixed bag of theories, which is understandable for something that is labelled "flexible" or "situationally relevant." In other words, it is the very fact of this mixture that unifies it as a new paradigm. Levy and Merry (1986) allude to this when they write that the OT consultant uses intervention technologies that are "open, emerging and mixed" (p. 91). When asked, during the study, "What is the single most distinguishing aspect, objective, or purpose of OT?", John Adams' immediate reply was lack of boundaries."

In the literature, Philip Harris (1985) describes organizations as "energy exchange systems" in which the inputs are physical, material, and psychic. According to the descriptions given by most of the participants in this study, many would agree with Harris' metaphor for organizations; some may substitute the word "psychic" with the words "mystic" or "spiritual," and others would perhaps say that the mystical, psychic, or spiritual aspects encompass the physical and material aspects.

Harris goes on to say that organizations are dynamic human systems with life cycles, in which they grow, expand, develop, stabilize, decline, and disappear—unless they are transformed and continually alter their forms. Most of the participants in this study describe organizations in a similar fashion. Harrison Owen, for example, states, "I'm really concerned with the full life cycle of the organization, which means starting from beginning through transformation in developmental stages." Owen also says in his description of Organization Transformation that an organization never becomes fully transformed, but must be in a continual process of transformation in order to survive in today's turbulent environment. And Allen Gordon says that Organization Transformation means continuous change, movement from one state of being to another, completely different state, without restrictions. "There's a flowingness about it."

Another key concept in the literature is that of Organization Transformation and Organization Development as working together in a complementary fashion rather than representing "either/or" alternatives. Levy and Merry (1986) point out several complementary elements of transformation and development and start by saying that Organization Transformation helps members to accept the need for second-order change and helps the organization to discover a new vision; whereas development helps the organization to plan and implement the change, and to elaborate the new vision in order to implement, legitimize and institutionalize it. In the same vein, Johnston (1987) describes OD and OT ideally working together:

An analogy illustrating how transformation and development work together is that of a baby who has been transporting him or herself solely on all fours, now rather suddenly stands holding on to a chair, and takes a wobbly step or two. This change we can call . . . transformation for the reason that the context, content and processes of experience appears to the child as a major shift from a 'crawling context' to an 'upright and walking context.' If the baby is to become an expert walker, even runner, his or her psycho-muscular coordination must be strengthened and refined. Such developmental processes usually require a considerable length of time. (p. 15)

One exciting discovery made by this study is that, in practice, most of the participants mix OT and OD technologies in a fashion similar to that described by Johnston (1987), and Levy and Merry (1986). Michael Shandler's "Vision Action" technology is one good example. He combines an Organization Transformation visioning technology with an Organization Development Action Research strategy that has worked surprisingly well in traditional midwestern smokestack industries.

The focus of this study has been specifically on the theorists and practitioners of Organization Transformation. The primary framing questions were: Who are these people? What are their underlying philosophical assumptions? What do they have in common that makes them an identifiable group of theorists and practitioners? On what points do they vary or differ? What do they think are the important contributions of OT? What impact do they predict that OT will have on organizations? Thus, the purpose of this study was to explore this new area of theory and practice (OT) by studying those who are developing and applying it.

All of the fourteen participants in this study are very active and busy professionals. They have a number of things going on at once, such as writing, teaching or lecturing, consulting, and various activities in professional and other organizations. Each person's story about how she or he became interested in Organization Transformation varies, and provides rich data for this study.

A wealth of data resulted from the interviews, all of which cannot possibly be discussed fully within the constraints of this book. However, all of the framing questions for the study were explored in-depth by means of the twenty-two interview questions.

Many insights and personal learnings have resulted from the study. One learning involves the categories of "theorists" and practitioners. It is clear that most of the participants in this study do not wish to categorize themselves using this framework, and they express a belief that OT practitioners must also be theorists, and conversely, theorists must have some practical experience. All but two of the participants represent themselves as some blend of theorist and practitioner.

Another important insight gained from the study concerns the definition of Organization Transformation presented in the first chapter:

Organization Transformation is an ecological, holistic, nonreductionistic, humanistic approach to radical, revolutionary, second-order change in the entire context of an organization's system. OT involves transformative changes in the fundamental nature of the organization in relation to its ecosystem, and requires completely new ways of thinking, behaving, and perceiving by members of the organization. OT strategies help the organization to be flexible and responsive to internal and external environments. OT strategies tend to intensify the organization's social consciousness and accordingly transform the organization's vision and mission.

Most of the participants agree that Organization Transformation involves radical, fundamental changes in organizational context, structure, and process. They also agree that a larger, systems perspective is required in OT, one which includes the organization's external environment. The major point on which they differ has to do with whether an organization can transform "negatively," as well as in a "positive" direction. However, it is interesting that, in response to the case, participants envision very positive, humanistically oriented outcomes for their interventions.

Most of the participants note that the reasons for the emergence of OT had to do with uncontrollable environmental and cultural trends, and several participants say that Organization Transformation is a natural process that has been happening all along. Overall, the findings from this study support the definition for OT put forth in Chapter 1.

The fifth question on the Interview Guide, "What is the single most distinguishing aspect, objective or purpose of OT?" elicited the widest variety of responses of the five questions in the "Meanings" section. Three of the responses have to do with participation of organization members. Two other responses seem to roughly correspond to the notion of universal connectedness. The remaining answers seem to vary, which suggests that there is no single, agreed upon distinguishing aspect of Organization Transformation.

However, several similar responses are given by different participants to the question "On what points do OT'ers agree?" They include fundamental organizational change, empowerment of organizational members, and human and systemic interconnections. To the question "On what points do OT'ers disagree?", many participants note that they would disagree about the "how to's," that is, the methods, approaches, strategies, and techniques for facilitating Organization Transformation.

Another insight has to do with the impact of Organization Transformation. Many participants express a belief that, thus far, the impact of Organization Transformation has been small; others say that the impact is currently negligible, but growing; and most express either a hope or a belief that the future impact will be great.

Another interesting learning has been that most participants believe that all organizations could benefit by OT, but some are more receptive to it than others.

Also, some participants sound very optimistic about the potential of Organization Transformation's impact on the current environment, while others are quite pessimistic. In addition, participants see current and future resistances to Organization Transformation coming from individuals, groups, and whole organizations, but primarily from individuals. The most common source of resistance is seen to be individuals fear of the unknown.

When questioned about what they do differently than other consultants, many participants talked about differences in underlying assumptions rather than actual practices. However, the two most common differences in interventions they cite are visioning and focusing on the total organization.

The case provided a rich source of information about what Organization Transformation practitioners actually do. Some of the methods, techniques, procedures and processes seem to be quite common among the fourteen participants, and others quite unique.

Perhaps the most interesting learning has been that most of the participants in this study mix what appear to be Organization Development techniques and OT concepts. For example, most of the participants use contracting, diagnosis, and feedback phases in their interventions that parallel the action research processes common in OD interventions. Also, many participants pay close attention to interpersonal interactions among the members of the hypothetical case organization that includes such things as team building and conflict resolution, both of which are common OD technologies.

One commonality among the participants' interventions is their recognition of something that transcends explanation. They give it different names; some call it "energy" or "joy," others refer to it as "commitment" and spirit."

Based on my interpretation of the context in which the participants in this study use the various themes emerging from the data, it seems clear that they could be described as possessing basic assumptions about their OT interventions that categorize those interventions as either uncontrollable, partially controllable, controllable, or situationally controllable. I surmise that it is very important for OT practitioners to examine their assumptions about the potential controllability of any change project they undertake.

I found this study to be intriguing, time-consuming, challenging, and even fun. The findings resulting from this study have far exceeded my expectations; they do not simply reflect theories that were already present in the literature, but extend into other themes going well beyond what was previously known. I met and talked with sixteen wonderful people who were very warm, open, and giving of their time—of themselves. I am pleased with the results of this study and have gleaned some valuable insights into the new phenomenon of Organization Transformation. If I were to do the study again, knowing what I know now in hindsight, there are a few things that I would do differently:

I would design the case as a common, hierarchical, autocratic, American business firm rather than an employee-owned operation. I wondered, during the course of the study, if the existing structure written into the case generated answers that would have been different had the situation been more common.

I would have asked more pointed questions about the advocacy of values in interventions. For example: "Do you have any personal, social, economic, or spiritual values that you want your clients to adopt? This would have given me more direct data on which to base a values analysis.

And, in that same vein, I would have asked a question about participants' assumptions regarding the controllability of transformational interventions in order to more directly test my ontologically based scheme for looking at the themes that emerged in the study.

Finally, there are some questions left unanswered by this study which are possible starting places for future studies of this nature

How would my results look if I had a larger sample?

What would be the effect of a different mix of participants as to race, gender, age, and geographic location?

I believe that the greatest power of the emerging new paradigm, Organization Transformation, is that it does not ignore issues that are experienced as the leading edge. It does not ignore questions that matter to people such as ethics, feelings, community, and the human spirit simply because they cannot be explained using traditional frames of reference (Vaill 1984). Organizational leaders can no longer ignore or fight the fast-paced turbulence they face in today's global society, nor can they hope to resolve fundamental issues by making superficial changes. A major shift in perspectives is necessary before they will experience relief. Unique and problematic situations are continually unfolding. Organizational Transformation theorists and practitioners can assist this unfolding by helping to reframe the turbulence in terms of opportunities for the future.

Appendices

Date _____ Time _____ Place _____
_____ Reviewed and signed Consent Form.
_____ Requested copy of resume.

Biographical Data

Name _____ Age _____
Current Position(s)/Title(s) _____
Organization(s) _____
Advanced Degree(s) _____
From what institution(s) _____

Meanings

1. What is the difference between "theorists" and "practitioners"?
   What are you—a theorist or a practitioner?

2. What does Organization Transformation mean to you—i.e., Your definition for OT?

3. What adjectives, nouns, metaphors or other descriptors would you use to describe an organization that has been transformed?

4. Why is there such a thing as OT?

5. What is the single most distinguishing aspect, objective or purpose of OT?

Background

6. How did you come to be interested in OT? Where has this interest in OT led you? (i.e., Are you a consultant, have you made any presentations, created any training packages, or produced any other creative works on the subject of OT?)

OT vs. OD

7. What is your definition for Organization Development (OD)?

8. Are there differences between OT and OD? If so, what are they?

OT'ers

9. What distinguishes an OT practitioner/theorist from other organizational practitioners/theorists?

10. On what points do OT'ers agree?

11. Disagree?

12. How do you fit into this picture?

Personal Philosophy

13. How would you summarize your philosophy about organizations?

14. Can you relate that to any particular school of thought or philosophy?

Consequences/Applicability

15. What impact has OT had; i.e., what are the contributions of OT?

16. What future impact do you predict that OT will have?

17. What are the current and possible future resistances to OT? From whom?

18. Is OT more applicable to certain types of domains and not applicable to others? Explain.

19. What are the potentials of OT, given our current social, economic and political systems?

Case (Read and ask questions at the end)

You have been called in to consult with a medium-size, Mid-Western member-owned organization that produces custom-designed office furniture.

This organization has been in operation since the early 1920s. What has made this company different is its dedication to the promotion of democratic management principles. Its primary decision-making body consists of a board of directors elected by its members. The chair of the board is selected by the members of the board, who serve in this position on a rotating basis.

For the past ten years, this organization's rate of growth has gradually decreased as more competitors have come into the market.

Internally, over the past ten years, the organization has experienced severe conflicts among its members over its mission, products, services, and general direction. The members of this organization have split into several powerful factions whose in-fighting has affected the quality of the organization's products and services.

20. How would you intervene in this particular situation? Describe your intervention.
21. What would you do differently from other consultants?
22. What outcomes would you expect from your intervention? Describe those outcomes.

Closure

23. What are your reactions to this case?
24. Are there any questions that you would have asked that I did not ask? (If so, request answer). Are there any questions you'd like to ask me?
25. Permission to follow-up/request for referrals.

Appendix B
Comparison of OD and OT Consultation Modes

	OD Consultant	OT Consultant
Emphasis:	Problems and dysfunctions in small groups and between groups	Functions and patterns in entire system
Approach:	Rational, analytic, deductive	Inductive, holistic, intuitive
Change Process:	Problem-solving	Pattern exchange
Intervention Technologies:	Structured, organized, step-by-step	Open, emerging, mixed
Diagnostic Tools:	Models, surveys, questionnaires	Ethnomethodological approaches

Source: Adapted from Levy and Merry, 1986, p. 91, by Fletcher 1988, Comp. Paper, p. 55.

Appendix C
The Complementary Elements of OT and OD

Organization Transformation	Organization Development
Helping members to accept the need for second-order change	Helping the organization to plan and implement the change
Helping the organization to discover and accept a new vision, a new world view, and to align members with this vision	Helping the organization to elaborate the new vision, to implement it, to legitimize and institutionalize it
Focusing on the first stages of second-order change	Focusing on the later stages of second-order change
Open; going with the client's needs, nonstructured, nonanalytical process	Rational, analytical, step-by-step, and collaborative process
Focusing on changes in individuals' consciousness	Focusing on changes in the interactions in the organization
Dealing with flow states and consciousness	Changing forms, procedures, roles, and structures
A process that might include moments of insight and a sudden shift in perceptions and behaviors	An incremental process that might include political campaign and conflicts
Facilitating and allowing	Managing and applying
Spirit and spirituality	Practicality, pragmatism
Energizing and empowering individuals, creating critical mass	Utilizing the organization's energy and resources for implementing the change
Allowing death and rebirth	Shaping the new form

Source: Adapted from Levy and Merry, 1986, p. 191, by Fletcher 1988, Comp. Paper, pp. 66–67.

Glossary

anti-positivism. Of an ontological nature, having to do with the nature of reality. What is real is not only that which is observable and measurable, but includes supersensory understanding and experiences.

change. 1a: to make different in some particular; b: to make radically different, transform; c: to give a different position, course, or direction; d: to undergo a loss or modification of (Webster's, 1983). There are basically three types of change: (1) *minor* = first-order, piecemeal, incremental, accommodative; (2) *major* = frame-bending "as new patterns develop, old ways of being are discarded, the whole system becomes involved, transformation may or may not occur; and (3) *transformative* = second-order, contextual, paradigmatic, discontinuous, frame-breaking, quantum, revolutionary, fundamenal, radical. A basic, radical, total change in an organization (Fletcher, 1988, p. 42).

deductive. Reasoning from a known principle to an unknown. From general to specific. From premise to logical conclusion. OD uses deductive logic.

determinism. 1. the doctrine that everything is entirely determined by a sequence of causes. 2. the doctrine that one's choice of action is not free, but is determined by a sequence of causes independent of her/his will. (Webster's, 1983)

disciplines. Included in OT: our traditional, mechanical, reductionistic world/view is being challenged by thinkers in many different disciplines (Fletcher, 1988, pgs. 36, 37 and 46):

Psychology or psychiatry. Charles Tart, Prof. of Psyc. at U.C. Davis; Herbert Benson, Researcher at Harvard Medical School; Roger Walsh, Prof. of Psychiatry at U.C. Irvine; Elmer Greene, Psycho-physiologist, Menninger Found; Alyce Greene, Researcher in Psychology, Menninger Found; Abraham Maslow, Psychologist–Pioneer Consciousness Research; Carl Jung, Psychiatrist; Roberto Assagioli, Psychiatrist–Psychosynthesis; and Barbara Brown, Psycho-physiologist, Prof. at UCLA.

Physics. David Bohm (Protegee of Einstein), work in Quantum Physics; Neils Bohr, Physicist; Sir Edward Sherrington, Physicist/Mystic; J. R. Oppenheimer, Physicist (theoretical); Einstein, Physicist ($E = MC^3$); and Werner Heisenberg, Physicist/Mystic "Uncertainty Principle" (listed in *The Medium, the Mystic and the Physicist* by LeShan).

Neuro Sciences. Carl Pribram, Stanford Medical School–Researcher; and Roger Sperry, Nobel Prize winner, Neuroscientist, Cal Tech.

Astronomy. Fred Hoyle, Astronomer, Physicist, *The Intelligent Universe.*

OD/OT. OT Network, former OD practitioner-founder: John Adams.

Engineering/Economics. Willis Harman (also research in psychology), *Global Mind Change.*

Chemistry. Psycho-pharmacology: psycho-chemical changes. Relationship of thought to chemical reactions—physiological changes in body—biofeedback measures show what happens when people act out love, fear, etc.

ecological. Of or by ecology. *Ecology* 1. the branch of *biology* that deals with the relations between living organisms and their environment. 2. In *sociology*, the relationship between the distribution of human groups with reference to material resources, and the consequent social and cultural patterns (Webster's, 1983). An ecological system has characteristics we would not have suspected by merely examining its component organisms—it is non-reductionistic (Fletcher, 1988, p. 19).

ecological psychology. An example of qualitative research traditions. It was developed by Roger Barker, Herbert Wright, and their colleagues at the University of Kansas. They drew heavily on natural history field studies and the work of Kurt Lewin. *Ecological psychologists* are interested in the relationships between human behavior and the environment—they see individuals and the environment as interdependent. They *assume* subjective aspects to behavior, which they examine in terms of goals. They also assume subjective aspects to the environment, which they usually discuss in terms of a person's emotional reactions to environment. They ask descriptive questions about either individuals' behavior and environment, or about the features of behavioral settings. One *focus* is individuals' perceived environment and goal-directed behavior, which they study using "specimen records. *Specimen record methodology*–nonparticipant observers write a narrative description of the behavior of one person over a substantial period of time. This "stream of behavior" is then divided into segments based on goal-directed actions. Coders draw upon their ordinary knowledge and perceptions to infer the goals that actors intend to achieve, marking off sections of narrative descriptions into segments leading toward specific goals. These segments are coded and analyzed *quantitatively*. Another *focus* is transindividual patterns of behavior associated w/particular constellations of places, things, and times, which they study using "behavior-setting surveys." *Behavior-setting surveys*–researchers identify all possible behavior settings and then identify those that meet stringent tests for true behavior settings. These are then coded for their features and analyzed quantitatively to provide a comprehensive description of all the behavior settings in a particular community or institution during a stated period of time (Jacob, 1988).

epistemology. The study of a theory of the nature and grounds of knowledge, especially with reference to its limits and validity. The theory or science that investigates the origin, nature, methods and limits of knowledge (Webster's, 1983). [See metaphysics]

ethnography. n. The branch of anthropology that deals descriptively with specific cultures (Webster's, 1983).

ethnography, holistic. An example of qualitative research traditions. Developed primarily from the work of Franz Boas and Bronislaw Malinowski. *Culture* a central concept—includes patterns *of* behavior and patterns *for* behavior. Patterns *for* behavior seen as systems of standards for deciding what is, what can be, how one feels about it, what to do about it, and how to go about doing it. These "standards" are seen as shared group phenomena leading to certain predictability in social life—but without determining behavior. *Holistic ethnographers assume* that certain aspects of human culture are central to understanding human life: social organization, economics, family structure, religion, politics, rituals, enculturation patterns, and ceremonial behavior. They also *assume* that the various aspects of a culture form a unique, unified whole, with the parts being interdependent. They *focus* on the study of the culture of bounded groups, with an interest in describing and analyzing the culture as a whole. Their goal is to describe a unique way of life, documenting the meanings attached to events and showing how the parts fit together into an integrated whole. They approach a particular culture with a minimum of preconceived ideas or theories beyond the general assumptions. Most holistic ethnographers gather empirical evidence directly themselves through "fieldwork, usually involving participant observations and informal interviews. They endeavor to document the participants' points of view, preferably through verbatim statements. They collect a wide range of data using a wide range of methods—analysis of the data is primarily qualitative (Jacob, 1988).

ethnomethodological approaches. From cultural anthropology: methods that compare culture, folklore, myths, symbols, etc., in the culture. Also, an example of qualitative research traditions (Jacob, 1988).

first-order change. A change within a given system which itself remains unchanged (Watzlawick, 1974). Those minor improvements and adjustments that do not change the system's core, and occur as the system naturally grows and develops (Levy and Merry, 1986).

functionalism. Theory or practice emphasizing the necessity of adapting the structure or design of anything to its function (Webster's, 1983).

holistic. Pertaining to holism. *holism* n. The view that an organic or integrated whole has a reality independent of and greater than the sum of its parts.

holistic ethnography. See ethnography, holistic.

ideographic. Belonging to, resembling, or containing an ideograph or ideographs. *ideograph*–to write. a characteristic signature or writing; one's own private mark; trademark (Webster's 1983).

inductive. Leading to inferences. The process of reasoning or drawing a conclusion from particular facts or individual cases (Webster's, 1983). Reasoning from the specific to the general. OT is inductive; qualitative research is inductive.

interpretive. 1. designed or used to explain; explaining; explanatory. 2. according to interpretation; constructive; inferential (Webster's, 1983).

metaphor. A transferring to one word the sense of another, from *metapherein*; *meta*, over, and *pherein*, to bear. A figure of speech in which one thing is likened to another, different thing by being spoken of as if it were that other; implied comparison, in which a word or phrase ordinarily and primarily used of one thing is applied to another (e.g., screaming headlines, "all the world's a stage"): distinguished from simile (Webster's, 1983).

metaphysics. 1. a division of philosophy that includes ontology and cosmology. 2. philosophy made up of ontology and epistemology. *metaphysical*–1. of or relating to metaphysics. 2a: of or relating to the transcendent or supersensible; b. supernatural; and c. highly abstract or abstruse.

nominalism. A doctrine of the late Middle Ages that all universal or abstract terms are mere necessities of thought or conveniences of language and therefore exist as names only and have no realities corresponding to them; opposed to (medieval) realism (Webster's, 1983).

nomothetic. 1. giving or enacting laws. 2. based on law. 3. of a science of general or universal laws (Webster's, 1983).

non-reductionistic. Phenomena cannot be explained in terms of elementary happenings. The whole does not equal the sum of its component parts; they don't add up.

objective. a. 1. of our having to do with a known or perceived object as distinguished from something existing only in the mind of the subject, or person thinking. 2. being, or regarded as being, independent of the mind; real; actual. 3. determined by and emphasizing the features and characteristics of the object, or thing dealt with, rather than the thoughts, feelings, etc. of the artist, writer, or speaker; as, an objective description, painting, etc. 4. without bias or prejudice; detached; impersonal. 5. being the aim or goal; as, an objective point.

objective. n. 1. anything external to or independent of the mind; something objective; reality. 2. something aimed at or striven for (Webster's, 1983).

objectivist. Of an epistemological nature (having to do with the nature and ground of knowledge). *Objectivist assumptions*: knowledge can only be explored by scientific inquiry using quantitative models to approximate the phenomenon progressively more precisely (Fletcher, 1988, p. 20).

ontology. A branch of metaphysics. The branch of metaphysics dealing with the nature of being or reality. The science of ontology comprehends investigations of every real existence, either beyond the sphere of the present world or in any other way incapable of being the direct object of consciousness, which can be deduced immediately from the possession of certain feelings or principles and faculties of the human soul (Archer Butler). *ontological*–relating to or based upon being or existence (Webster's, 1983).

organization. 4. any unified, consolidated group of elements; systematized whole; especially, a body of persons organized for some specific purpose, as a club, union, or society. 5. the administrative personnel or executive structure of a business. 6. all the functionaries, committees, etc. of a political party (Webster's, 1983). The simplest definition of organization, and one perhaps most useful here is: two or more people gathered for a common purpose (Fletcher, 1988, p. 15).

Organization Development (OD). A primarily behavioral science approach to planned organizational change that is composed of Traditional OD and Mainline OD (Krell, 1981) as follows:

Traditional OD. Humanistic orientation; Laboratory training/group dynamics; Survey research/feedback; and Action Research.

Mainline OD. Concerned with productivity; and Socio-technical processes.

The *primary focus* of OD interventions is on small groups, teams, or specific sections of the organization.

Organizational Transformation (OT). An *ecological, holistic,* approach to *radical, revolutionary, second-order* change in the *entire* context of the organization's system [from a humanistic perspective]. This involves transformative changes in the fundamental nature of the organization and requires completely new ways of thinking, behaving, and perceiving by members of the organization. OT strategies help the organization to be *flexible and responsive* to internal and external environments. OT strategies transform the organization's vision and mission (Fletcher, 1988).

paradigm. A pattern, example, or model (Webster's 1983). A way of viewing the world, a conceptual framework, a guide for making sense of things, a way to define truth and reality. It is a collection of techniques, processes, values, ideas, and beliefs shared by the members of a given community. It is, furthermore, a belief system that does not, and cannot, fully represent total reality (Fletcher, 1988, p. 16).

pluralism. In philosophy, the theory that reality is composed of a multiplicity of ultimate beings, principles, or substances: it opposes the position of monism that reality is ultimately one, but agrees in denying the dualism of mind and body (Webster's, 1983).

positivism. 1. the quality or state of being positive; certainty; assurance. 2. dogmatism. 3. a system of philosophy based solely on the positive data of sense experience; empiricism; especially a system of philosophy, originated by Auguste Comte, which is based solely on positive, observable, scientific facts and their relations to each other and to natural law: it rejects speculation on or search for ultimate origins (Webster's, 1983). Of an *ontological* nature—having to do with the nature of reality. A *positivist assumption* is: only that which is physically observable is real (Fletcher, 1988, p. 20). What is real (or at least discussible) is taken to be that which can be measured—that is, what is ultimately discernible to the physical senses, either directly or by the use of scientific instrumentation (Harman, 1988).

profile. Outline; as, the profile of a distant hill. A short, vivid biography, briefly outlining the most outstanding characteristics of the subject (Webster's, 1983).

quantum. In the quantum theory, a fixed, elemental unit, as of energy, angular momentum, etc. *quantum jump* (or leap); (a) a sudden alteration in the energy level of an atom or molecule, together with the emission or absorption of radiant energy; (b) any sudden and extensive change or advance, as in a program or policy (Webster's, 1983).

realism. n. 1. a tendency to face facts and be practical rather than imaginary or visionary. 2. in art and literature, the attempted picturing of people and things as they really are; effort at faithful reproduction of nature. 3. in philosophy, (a) the doctrine that universals have objective reality: opposed to nominalism; (b) the doctrine that material objects exist in themselves, apart from the mind's consciousness of them: opposed to idealism (Webster's, 1983).

reductionism. Scientists have sought to explain phenomena in terms of more elementary happenings (for example, color explained in terms of wavelength, gas pressure in terms of the motion of the gas molecules (Harman, 1988). That is, the whole is equal to the sum of its parts.

second-order change. A change whose occurrence changes the system itself (Watzlawick, 1974). Also referred to as Organization Transformation—a multidimensional, multi-level, qualitative, discontinuous, radical organizational change involving a paradigmatic shift (Levy and Merry, 1986).

structuralist. n. a follower or advocate of structural principles, as in the analysis or application of social, economic, or linguistic theory. *structuralism* n. 1. a movement for determining and analyzing the basic, relatively stable structural elements of a system, especially in the behavioral sciences (Webster's, 1988).

subjective. a.–1. of, affected by, or produced by the mind or a particular state of mind; of or resulting from the feelings or temperament of the subject, or person thinking, rather than the attributes of the object thought of; as, a subjective judgment. 2. determined by and emphasizing the ideas, thoughts, feelings, etc., of the artist, writer, or speaker. 3. in grammar, nominative. 4. in philosophy, having to do with any of the elements in apprehension or apperception derived from the limitations of the mind rather than from reality independent of mind. 5. in medicine, designating or of a symptom or condition perceptible only to the patient. 6. in psychology, (a) existing or originating within the observer's mind and, hence, incapable of being checked externally or verified by other persons; (b) introspective (Webster's, 1983).

symbol. Something that stands for or represents another thing; especially, an object used to represent something abstract; an emblem; as the dove is a symbol of peace, the cross is the symbol of Christianity (Webster's, 1983).

symbolic interactionism. Developed by Herbert Blumer, drawing on the work of G. H. Mead, Charles Cooley, John Dewey, and W. I. Thomas. Symbolic interactionists see humans as qualitatively different from other animals. Nonhuman animals act in response to other objects and events based on factors such as instinct or previous conditioning—humans act based on meanings those objects have for them. Symbolic interactionists *assume* that meanings arise through social interaction, but that an individual's use of meanings is not automatic. The actor selects, checks, suspends, regroups, and transforms the meanings in the light of the situation in which she or he is placed and the direction of her/his action. They do not see macro structures as having a life of their own. Human society is to be seen as consisting of acting people, and the life of the society is to be seen as consisting of their actions. They are interested in understanding the *processes* involved in symbolic interaction. They seek to know how individuals take one another's perspective and learn meanings and symbols in concrete instances of interaction. *Data* collection: primarily participant observation and open interviews. They also collect life histories, autobiographies, case studies, and letters. Analysis of these data is usually qualitative (Jacob, 1988).

theme. A subject or topic on which a person writes or speaks; anything proposed as a subject of discussion or discourse; as, the speaker made education his theme. A subject or topic of discourse or of artistic representation (Webster's, 1983).

theory. From Gr. *theoria*, a looking at, contemplation, speculation, theory. Originally, a mental viewing; contemplation. An idea or mental plan of the way to do something.

A systematic statement of principles involved; as, the theory of equations in mathematics. A formulation of apparent relationships or underlying principles of certain observed phenomena which has been verified to some degree: distinguished from hypothesis (Webster's, 1983).

third-order change. The kind of "permanent" change that comes when one discovers his or her essential oneness with whole-mind consciousness and uses it as a permanent, stable home base of consciousness for making second-order and first-order changes which can be done with lucidity, health, freedom, genius, and facility without losing one's sense of center and equilibrium (Johnston, 1987).

transformation. [Also see Organization Transformation]. 1. the act or operation of changing the form or external appearance; the state of being transformed; a change in form, appearance, nature, disposition, condition, character, etc. 2. in biology, change of form in insects; metamorphosis, as from a catepillar to a butterfly. 3. in alchemy, the change of one metal into another; transmutation of metals (Webster's, 1983).

transformative change. Second-order and/or third-order contextual, paradigmatic, discontinuous, frame-breaking, quantum, revolutionary, fundamental, radical. A basic, radical, total change in an organization (Fletcher, 1988, p. 43).

voluntarism. n. in philosophy, a theory which holds that reality is ultimately of the nature of will or that the will is the primary factor in experience (Webster's, 1983).

Bibliography

Ackerman, Linda S. (April 1986). "Change Management: Basics for Training," *Training and Development Journal*, V. 40, p. 67 (2).

Ackerman, Linda S. (1984). "The Flow State: A New View of Organizations and Managing," in *Transforming Work: A Collection of Organizational Transformation Readings*. Alexandria, VA: Miles River Press.

Adams, John D. (June 1988). "Creating Critical Mass to Support Change," *OD Practitioner*, p. 7 (4).

Adams, John D. (1987). *The Role of the Creative Outlook in Team Building*. Winchester, VA: Eartheart Enterprises.

Adams, John D. (1989). [Interview Transcript for Doctoral Dissertation: *Organization Transformation Theorists and Practitioners: Profiles and Themes* by B. R. Fletcher]. Unpublished raw data.

Adams, John D., ed. (1986). *Transforming Leadership*. Alexandria, VA: Miles River Press.

Adams, John D., ed. (1984). *Transforming Work: A Collection of Organizational Transformation Readings*. Alexandria, VA: Miles River Press.

Adams, John D. and Spencer, Sabina (1986). "Consulting with the Strategic Leadership Perspective," *Consultation*, V. 5, No. 3, p. 149 (11).

Adams, John D. and Spencer, Sabina (1986). *Strategic Direction*. Winchester, VA: Eartheart Enterprises. Oct., No. 12.

Allen, Robert F. and Kraft, Charlotte (1984). "Transformations that Last: A Cultural Approach," in *Transforming Work: A Collection of Organizational Transformation Readings*. Ed. John D. Adams. Alexandria, VA: Miles River Press.

Anderson, Norma Jean (1989). [Interview Transcript for Doctoral Dissertation: *Organization Transformation Theorists and Practitioners: Profiles and Themes*, by B. R. Fletcher]. Unpublished raw data.

Bartunek, Jean M. (1984). "Changing Interpretive Schemes and Organizational Restructuring: The Example of a Religious Order," *Administrative Science Quarterly*, Sept., pp. 355–372.

Bartunek, Jean M. (1988). "The Dynamics of Personal and Organizational Reframing," in *Paradox and Transformation: Toward a Theory of Change in Organization and Management*. R. E. Quinn and K. S. Cameron Eds., Cambridge, MA: Ballinger.

Bartunek, Jean M. (1989). [Interview Transcript for Doctoral Dissertation: *Organization Transformation Theorists and Practitioners: Profiles and Themes*, by B. R. Fletcher]. Unpublished raw data.

Bartunek, Jean M. and Franzak, Frank J. (1988). "The Effects of Organizational Restructuring on Frames of Reference and Cooperation," *Journal of Management*. V. 14, No. 4, pp. 579–592.

Bartunek, Jean M. and Louis, Meryl R. (1988). "The Interplay of Organization Development and Organizational Transformation," *Research in Organizational Change and Development*, V. 2, pp. 97–134.

Bartunek, Jean M. and Moch, Michael K. (1987). "First-Order, Second-Order, and Third-Order Change and Organization Development Interventions: A Cognitive Approach," *The Journal of Applied Behavioral Science*, V. 23, No. 4, pp. 483–500.

Bartunek, Jean M. and Reid, Robin D. (August 1988). "Expressions and Effects of Conflict During Second-Order Change." In D. Kolb & R. Lewicki (Chairs), *The Cultural Contexts of Organizational Conflict*. Symposium conducted at the Academy of Management meeting, Anaheim, CA.

Beck, Arthur C. and Hillmar, Ellis D. (1986). *Positive Management Practices*. San Francisco, CA: Jossey-Bass.

Beckhard, Richard. (1988) "The Executive Management of Transformational Change." In *Corporate Transformation: Revitalizing Organizations for a Competitive World*. Eds. Ralph Kilmann and Teresa Covin & Assoc. San Francisco, CA: Jossey-Bass.

Beckhard, Richard (1969). *Organizational Development: Strategies and Models*. Reading, MA: Addison-Wesley.

Beer, Michael (1988). "The Critical Path for Change: Keys to Success and Failure in Six Companies." In *Corporate Transformation: Revitalizing Organizations for a Competitive World*. San Francisco, CA: Jossey-Bass.

Beer, Michael (1980). *Organization Change and Development: A Systems View*. Santa Monica, CA: Goodyear Pub. Co.

Belgard, William P.; Fisher, K. Kim; and Rayner, Steven R. (1988). "Vision, Opportunity, and Tenacity: Three Informal Processes that Influence Formal Transformation." In *Corporate Transformation: Revitalizing Organizations for a Competitive World*. Eds. Ralph Kilmann and Teresa Covin & Assoc. San Francisco, CA: Jossey-Bass.

Bennis, Warren G. (1966). *Changing Organizations: Essays on the Development and Evolution of Human Organizations*. New York: McGraw-Hill, Inc.

Bennis, Warren G. (1969). *Organization Development: Its Nature, Origins, and Prospects*. Reading, Mass: Addison-Wesley.

Beres, Mary Elizabeth and Musser, Steven J. (1988). "Avenues and Impediments to Transformation: Lessons from a Case of Bottom-up Change," In *Corporate Transformation: Revitalizing Organizations for a Competitive World*. Eds. Ralph Kilmann and Teresa Covin & Assoc. San Francisco, CA: Jossey-Bass.

Blake, Robert R. and Mouton, Jane Srygley. (1988). "Comparing Strategies for Incremental and Transformational Change." In *Corporate Transformation: Revitalizing Organizations for a Competitive World*. Eds. Ralph Kilmann and Teresa Covin & Assoc. San Francisco, CA: Jossey-Bass.

Bohm, David (1980). *Wholeness and the Implicate Order*, London, England: ARK.

Bolman, Lee G. and Deal, Terrence E. (1984). *Modern Approaches to Understanding and Managing Organizations*. San Francisco, CA: Jossey-Bass Inc.

Bowey, Angela M. (Fall 1983). "Myths and Theories of Organization." *International Studies of Management & Organization*, V. 13, pp. 69–91.

Buckley, Karen Wilhelm and Perkins, Dani (1984). "Managing the Complexity of Organizational Transformation." In *Transforming Work: A Collection of Organizational Transformation Readings*. Ed. John D. Adams. Alexandria, VA: Miles River Press.

Burgess, Robert G. (1984). *The Research Process in Educational Settings: Ten Case Studies*. London: The Falmer Press.

Buckart, Michael (1989). [Interview Transcript for Doctoral Dissertation: *Organization Transformation Theorists and Practitioners: Profiles and Themes*, by B. R. Fletcher]. Unpublished raw data.

Burrell, Gibson and Morgan, Gareth (1979). *Sociological Paradigms and Organisational Analysis: Elements of the Sociology of Corporate Life*. London: Heinemann.

Capra, Fritjof (1977). *The Tao of Physics*. New York: Bantam Books, Inc.

Carew, Donald K. (1989) [Interview Transcript for Doctoral Dissertation: *Organization Transformation Theorists and Practitioners: Profiles and Themes*, by B. R. Fletcher]. Unpublished raw data.

Connelly, Sharon L. (May 5, 1984). *Work Spirit: Recapturing the Vitality of Work*. A conference presentation for the Association of Humanistic Psychology Conference on "People and Work: Excitement and Growth in the Workplace." Gutman Conference Center, Cambridge, MA. Conference materials copyright: Resource Development Systems, Arlington, Virginia.

Cook, Karen (September 25, 1988). "Scenario for a New Age." *The New York Times Magazine*, The Business World, p. 27 (5).

de Bivort, Lawrence H. (1984). "Fast-Tracking the Transformation of Organizations." In *Transforming Work: A Collection of Organizational Transformation Readings*. Ed. John D. Adams. Alexandria, VA: Miles River Press.

Dyer, William G. and Dyer, Gibb, Jr. (February 1986). "Organization Development: System Change or Culture Change?" *Personnel*, V. 63, p. 14 (8).

Dyer, William G. (April 1981). "Selecting an Intervention for Organization Change." *Training & Development Journal*, V. 35, pp. 62–66.

Esty, Katharine (1988). "Group Methods for Transformation." In *Corporate Transformation: Revitalizing Organizations for a Competitive World*. Eds. Ralph Kilmann and Teresa Covin & Assoc. San Francisco, CA: Jossey-Bass.

Esty, Katharine (1989). [Interview Transcript for Doctoral Dissertation: *Organization Transformation Theorists and Practitioners: Profiles and Themes*, by B. R. Fletcher]. Unpublished raw data.

Finney, Michael; Bowen, David E.; Pearson, Christine M.; and Siehl, Caren (1988). "Designing Blueprints for Organizationwide Transformation." In *Corporate Transformation: Revitalizing Organizations for a Competitive World*. Eds. Ralph Kilmann and Teresa Covin & Assoc. San Francisco, CA: Jossey-Bass.

Fletcher, Beverly R. (February 1988). *Organization Change, Transformation, and Development; an Overview of the Literature*. Unpublished manuscript presented to Comprehensive Qualifying Exam Committee, University of Massachusetts at Amherst, School of Education.

Fletcher, Beverly R. (1988). *Organization Transformation: A New Paradigm*. Unpublished manuscript submitted to Comprehensive Qualifying Examination Committee, University of Massachusetts at Amherst, School of Education.

French, Wendell L. (1982). "The Emergence and Early History of Organization Development." *Group & Organization Studies*, V. 7, pp. 261–278.

Gemmill, Gary and Smith, Charles (August 1985). "A Dissipative Structure Model of Organization Transformation." *Human Relations*, V. 38, pp. 751–766.

Goodman, Paul S. and Associates (1982). *Change in Organizations*. 1st ed. San Francisco: Jossey-Bass.

Gordon, Allen (1989). [Interview Transcript for Doctoral Dissertation: *Organization Transformation Theorists and Practitioners: Profiles and Themes*, by B. R. Fletcher]. Unpublished raw data.

Grof, Stanislav (1985). *Beyond the Brain: Birth, Death and Transcendence in Psychotherapy*. New York: State University of New York Press.

Hanna, Robert W. (1985). "Personal Meaning: Its Loss and Rediscovery." In *Human Systems Development: New Perspectives on People and Organizations*. Eds. Robert Tannenbaum et al. San Francisco, CA: Jossey-Bass.

Harman, Willis (1988). *Global Mind Change: The Promise of the Last Years of the Twentieth Century*. Indianapolis, Indiana: Knowledge Systems, Inc.

Harman, Willis and Rheingold, Howard (1984). *Higher Creativity: Liberating the Unconscious for Breakthrough Insights*. Los Angeles, CA: Jeremy P. Tarcher, Inc.

Harrigan, Kathryn R. (1985). *Strategic Flexibility: A Management Guide For Changing Times*. Lexington, MA: Lexington Books.

Harris, Philip R. (1985). *Management in Transition: Transforming Managerial Practices and Organizational Strategies for a New Work Culture*. San Francisco: Jossey-Bass.

Harris, Philip R. (1983). *New World, New Ways, New Management*. NY: American Management Association.

Hayes, Roger and Watts, Reginald (1986). *Corporate Revolution*. London: Heinemann.

Holvino, Evangelina (1989). [Interview Transcript for Doctoral Dissertation: *Organization Transformation Theorists and Practitioners: Profiles and Themes*, by B. R. Fletcher]. Unpublished raw data.

Ingle, Grant (1989). [Interview Transcript for Doctoral Dissertation: *Organization Transformation Theorists and Practitioners: Profiles and Themes*, by B. R. Fletcher]. Unpublished raw data.

Ingle, Grant (1989). *Placing the "Valuing Differences" Approach in a Campus Setting: Complexity and Challenge*. Unpublished manuscript, University of Massachusetts at Amherst, Office of Human Relations.

Jacob, Evelyn (January 1988). "Clarifying Qualitative Research: A Focus on Traditions." *Educational Researcher*, pp. 16–24.

Johnston, Robert W. (January 1988). *An Outline of Wholeminded Change Theory.* Unpublished paper.

Johnston, Robert W. (September 1985). "A Path to Whole Organization Transformation and Development." *Vision/Action Journal.*

Johnston, Robert W. (Winter 1987). "Integrating Organization Development With Spirituality." *Journal of Religion and the Applied Behavioral Sciences*, pp. 5–9.

Johnston, Robert W. (1989). [Interview Transcript for Doctoral Dissertation: *Organization Transformation Theorists and Practitioners: Profiles and Themes*, by B. R. Fletcher]. Unpublished raw data.

Johnston, Robert W. (January 1979). "Seven Steps to Whole Organization Development." *Training & Development Journal*, V. 33, No. 1, pp. 12–22.

Johnston, Robert W. (Copyright, 1987). *Toward a General Theory of Whole Mind Consciouosness: Freest Foundation For Self-Mastery, Genius, Personal and Organization Change, Transformation and Development—An Overview.*

Kast, Fremont E. and Rosenzweig, James E. (1979). *Organization and Management: A Systems and Contingency Approach.* New York: McGraw-Hill, Inc.

Keidel, Robert W. (November 1981). "Theme Appreciation as a Construct for Organizational Change." *Management Science*, V. 27, pp. 1261–1278.

Kiefer, Charles and Stroh, Peter (April 1983). "A New Paradigm for Organization Development." *Training & Development Journal*, V. 37, pp. 26–28.

Kilmann, Ralph H. and Covin, Teresa Joyce (1988). *Corporate Transformation: Revitalizing Organizations for a Competitive World.* San Francisco, CA: Jossey-Bass.

Koolhaas, Jan (1982). *Organization Dissonance and Change.* New York: Wiley Press.

Krell, Terence C. (September 1981). "The Marketing of Organization Development: Past, Present, and Future." *The Journal of Applied Behavioral Science*, V. 17, No. 3, pp. 309–328.

Kueppers, William G. (1976). *Colloquium Project: My Own Self as a Valid Object for Academic Study; An Inner Journey; Love of Self and Fellow Man.* Unpublished manuscripts, St. Mary's College, Human Development, Winona, Minn.

Kueppers, William G. (1989). [Interview Transcript for Doctoral Dissertation: *Organization Transformation Theorists and Practitioners: Profiles and Themes*, by B. R. Fletcher]. Unpublished raw data.

LaFerriere, Constance (1989). *Volunteering: An Interview Study of Women Leaders in a Liberal Religious Organization.* Amherst, MA: University of Massachusetts.

Lawler, Edward E. III (1988). "Transformation from Control to Involvement." In *Corporate Transformation: Revitalizing Organizations for a Competitive World.* Eds. Ralph Kilmann and Teresa Covin & Assoc. San Francisco, CA: Jossey-Bass.

Levy, Amir and Merry, Uri (1986). *Organizational Transformation; Approaches, Strategies, Theories.* New York: Praeger Publishers.

Lindsey, Robert (September 29, 1986). "Spiritual Concepts Drawing A Different Breed of Adherent." *The New York Times* (Special), p. A1.

Lippitt, Gordon L. (1982). *Organizational Renewal: A Holistic Approach to Organization Development.* 2nd ed. Englewood Cliffs, N.J.: Prentice-Hall.

Lippitt, Gordon L. (1973). *Visualizing Change; Model Building and the Change Process.* Fairfax, VA: NTL Learning Resources Corp.

Lorsch, Jay W. (Winter 1986). "Managing Culture: The Invisible Barrier to Strategic Change. *California Management Review*, V. 28, p. 95 (15).

Martel, Leon (1986). *Mastering Change: The Key to Business Success.* New York: Simon & Schuster.

Michael, Stephen R; Luthans, Fred; Odiorne, George S.; Burke, W. Warner; and Hayden, Spencer (1981). *Techniques of Organizational Change.* New York: McGraw-Hill.

Miles, Matthew B. and Huberman, A. Michael (1984). *Qualitative Data Analysis; A Sourcebook of New Methods.* Beverly Hills, CA: Sage.

Miller, Danny and Friesen, Peter H. (1984). *Organizations: A Quantum View.* Englewood Cliffs, N.J.: Prentice-Hall.

Moore, Maggie and Gergen, Paul (1988). "Turning the Pain of Change into Creativity and Structure for the New Order." In *Corporate Transformation: Revitaliziang Organizations for a Competitive World.* Eds. Ralph Kilmann and Joyce Covin & Assoc. San Francisco, CA: Jossey-Bass.

Morgan, Gareth, ed. (1983). *Beyond Method: Strategies for Social Research.* Beverly Hills, CA: Sage.

Morgan, Gareth (1986). *Images of Organization.* Beverly Hills, CA: Sage.

Nadler, David A. (1988). "Organizational Frame Bending: Types of Change in the Complex Organization." In *Corporate Transformation: Revitalizing Organizations for a Competitive World.* Eds. Ralph Kilmann and Teresa Covin & Assoc. San Francisco, CA: Jossey-Bass.

Naisbitt, John (1982). *Megatrends; Ten New Directions Transforming Our Lives*, New York: Warner Books, Inc.

Nelson, Linda and Burns, Frank L. (1984). "High Performance Programming: A Framework for Transforming Organizations." In *Transforming Work: A Collection of Organizational Transformation Readings.* Ed. John D. Adams. Alexandria, VA: Miles River Press.

Owen, Harrison (1989). *The Business of Business is Learning.* Potomac, MD: H. H. Owen & Co.

Owen, Harrison (1984). "Facilitating Organizational Transformation: The Uses of Myth and Ritual." In *Transforming Work: A Collection of Organizational Transformation Readings.* Ed. John D. Adams. Alexandria, VA: Miles River Press.

Owen, Harrison (1989). [Interview Transcript for Doctoral Dissertation: *Organization Transformation Theorists and Practitioners: Profiles and Themes*, by B. R. Fletcher]. Unpublished raw data.

Owen, Harrison (1989). *Organizations with Spirit.* Potomac, MD: H. H. Owen & Co.

Owen, Harrison (1989). *Spirit at Work.* Unpublished manuscript.

Owen, Harrison (1987). *Spirit: Transformation and Development in Organizations*, Potomac, Md: Abbott Publishing.

Owen, Harrison (1989). *Transformation Now and Then*, invitation to the Seventh Annual Symposium on Organization Transformation (OTVII), to be held July 1989, Madison, WI.

Patton, Michael Quinn (1980). *Qualitative Evaluation Methods.* Beverly Hills: Sage.

Perkins, Dani and Buckley, Karen W. (1985). "Transformative Change." In *How to Manage Change Effectively.* Ed. Donald L. Kirkpatrick. San Francisco, CA: Jossey-Bass.

Ray, Michael and Myers, Rochelle (1986). *Creativity in Business.* Garden City, New York: Doubleday & Co.

Reed, Horce B. and Loughran, Elizabeth Lee, eds. (1984). *Beyond Schools; Education for Economic, Social and Personal Development.* Amherst, MA: Citizen Involvement Training Program, Community Education Resource Center, School of Education, University of Massachusetts.

Roitman, David B.; Liker, Jeffrey K.; and Roskies, Ethel (1988). "Birthing a Factory of the Future: When is 'All at Once' Too Much?" In *Corporate Transformation: Revitalizing Organizations for a Competitive World.* Eds. Ralph Kilmann and Teresa Covin & Assoc. San Francisco, CA: Jossey-Bass.

Rollins, Bryant (1989). [Interview Transcript for Doctoral Dissertation: *Organization Transformation Theorists and Practitioners: Profiles and Themes,* by B. R. Fletcher]. Unpublished raw data.

Rollins, Bryant (1988). *Partners in Chaos: The Joy, Excitement, Pain and Danger of Managing the New Cultural Diversity in the American Workplace and Society.* Hartsdale, NY: Mountaintop Ventures, Inc.

Sargent, Alice G. (1981). *The Androgynous Manager.* New York: AMACOM.

Schein, Edgar H. (1985). *Organizational Culture and Leadership.* 1st ed. San Francisco: Jossey-Bass.

Shandler, Michael (1989). [Interview Transcript for Doctoral Dissertation: *Organization Transformation Theorsits and Practitioners: Profiles and Themes,* by B. R. Fletcher]. Unpublished raw data.

Shandler, Michael (1986). "Leadership and the Art of Understanding Structure," in *Transforming Leadership.* Ed. John D. Adams. Alexandria, VA: Miles River Press.

Shandler, Michael (1989). *Planning for Inspired Performance; A Program for Creating a Desired Organizational Future.* Amherst, MA: Vision-Action Associates.

Simmons, John (1989). [Interview Transcript for Doctoral Dissertation: *Organization Transformation Theorists and Practitioners: Profiles and Themes,* by B. R. Fletcher]. Unpublished raw data.

Simmons, John and Karasik, Judy (October 11, 1987). "GM's Corporate Tuneup," *The Boston Globe Magazine.*

Skibbins, Gerald J. (1974). *Organizational Evolution; a Program for Managing Radical Change.* New York: AMACOM.

Smith, Kenwyn K. and Berg, David N. (1987). *Paradoxes of Group Life,* San Francisco, CA: Jossey-Bass.

Smith, Kenwyn K. (1982). "Philosophical Problems in Thinking About Organizational Change. In *Change in Organizations: New Perspectives on Theory, Research, and Practice.* Author: Paul S. Goodman & Assoc. San Francisco, CA: Jossey-Bass.

Spencer, Sabina A. and Adams, John D. (October 1988). "People in Transition," *Training & Development Journal,* pp. 61–63.

Spradley, James P. (1979). *The Ethnographic Interview.* New York: Holt, Rinehart and Winston.

Spradley, James P. (1980). *Participant Observation.* New York: Holt, Rinehart and Winston.

Stetson-Kessler, Shirley (1989). [Interview Transcript for Doctoral Dissertation: *Organization Transformation Theorists and Practitioners: Profiles and Themes,* by B. R. Fletcher]. Unpublished raw data.

Taylor, Steven J. and Bogdan, Robert (1984). *Introduction to Qualitative Research Methods: The Search for Meanings.* 2nd ed. New York: John Wiley & Sons.

Tichy, Noel M. and Devanna, Mary Anne (1986). *The Transformational Leader*. New York: John Wiley & Sons.

Tushman, Michael L.; Newman, William H.; and Nadler, David A. (1988). "Executive Leadership and Organizational Evolution: Managing Incremental and Discontinuous Change." In *Corporate Transformation: Revitalizing Organizations for a Competitive World*. Eds. Ralph Kilmann and Teresa Covin & Assoc. San Francisco, CA: Jossey-Bass.

Vaill, Peter B. (1984). "Process Wisdom for a New Age." In *Transforming Work: A Collection of Organizational Transformation Readings*. Alexandria, VA: Miles River Press.

Veltrop, Bill and Harrington, Karin. (1988). "Proven Technologies for Transformation." In *Corporate Transformation: Revitalizing Organizations for a Competitive World*. Eds. Ralph Kilmann and Teresa Covin. San Francisco, CA: Jossey-Bass.

Webster's New Universal Unabridged Dictionary, 2nd ed. (1983), New York: New World Dictionaries/Simon & Schuster.

Weisbord, Marvin R. (1986). "Toward Third-Wave Managing and Consulting." *Organizational Dynamics*, pp. 5-24.

White, Orion F. Jr. and McSwain, Cynthia J. (1983). "Transformational Theory and Organizational Analysis." In *Beyond Method*, by Gareth Morgan. Beverly Hills, CA: Sage Publications.

Wolcott, H. F. (1975). "Criteria for an Ethnographic Approach to Research in Schools." *Human Organization*, 34: 111–128.

Wolcott, H. F. (1985). "On Ethnographic Intent." *Educational Administrative Quarterly*, 21 (3), pp. 187–203.

Index

Triage, and transformation, 76
Triune relationship, as essence, 45–46, 72
Trusts, in organizations, 63, 73

Unconsciousness Stage, of transformative change, 11
Universal Theory, of OT, 135
University, and change, 39
Unfreezing, in transformation phase, 13
Urban League, 55

Values, in OT context, 10, 22, 27, 30, 42–43, 59, 62, 66, 70, 73, 77, 82, 102
Viability, of organizations, 75
Vision, in intervention, 13; and OT, 19, 23, 37, 41, 56–57, 59, 74, 79, 82, 84, 99, 107

Vision Action Technology, in transformation, 137
Vision statements: in corporations, 97
Visionaries, in change, 13
Visionary Goal Champions, in change, 60
Veterans Administration, 48
Vows, in religious orders, 28

Whole-system change, effects of, 5
Wilbur, Ken, 72, 80
Work, problems and potentialities, 2, 73, 95–96, 98
World Marketplace, and OT, 3
Women, and OT, 99–100, 107
Women's Education Equity Project, 38

Yin and Yang, 72

ABOUT THE AUTHOR

BEVERLY R. FLETCHER is an educator, researcher, consultant, and professional manager. She specializes in practical self- and organization transformation and development concepts, processes, and applications. These include approaches to helping individuals, groups, and organizations to enhance their creativity, competence, teamwork, productivity, and prosperity.

Dr. Fletcher has experience in the education, entertainment, finance, public utility, and city and county government sectors of the economy. She has consulting and professional management experience with planning, general services, accounting, and information systems organizations. She is currently a member of the Western New England Organization Development Network (ODN), The Organization Transformation Network (OTN), and the National Training Laboratories (NTL).